# the
# promise

# Also by Mandy Morris

*8 Secrets to Powerful Manifesting: How
to Create the Reality of Your Dreams* *

*Love "It's How I Manifest": On Abundance,
Happiness, Joy, and Peace of Mind*

*\*Available from Hay House*

Please visit:

Hay House USA: www.hayhouse.com®
Hay House Australia: www.hayhouse.com.au
Hay House UK: www.hayhouse.co.uk
Hay House India: www.hayhouse.co.in

# the
# promise

## Break Free from Limitation and Reclaim Your Inner Power

## by Mandy Morris

HAY HOUSE, INC.
Carlsbad, California • New York City
London • Sydney • New Delhi

Cataloging-in-Publication Data is on file at the Library of Congress

Hardcover ISBN: 978-1-4019-7545-6
E-book ISBN: 978-1-4019-7546-3
Audiobook ISBN: 978-1-4019-7547-0

10  9  8  7  6  5  4  3  2  1

1st edition, March 2024

Printed in the United States of America

SUSTAINABLE
FORESTRY
INITIATIVE

Certified Chain of Custody
Promoting Sustainable Forestry

www.forests.org
SFI-01268

SFI label applies to the text stock

This product uses papers sourced from responsibly managed forests. For
more information, see www.hayhouse.com.

*To my children,*

*with me in body and in spirit*

# contents

# introduction

Hello, beautiful soul.

You are about to embark on a journey unlike one you've ever experienced, a powerful crash course in accessing your light, which is the source of your authentic self.

Every day, I meet incredibly intelligent, self-aware people who need that extra nudge in order to express their potential in the world and fully experience the joy and wonder that are possible when they come to live in and from the light. You have a personal story that is part of a larger web called the human story, and some of the smartest, most sincere and awakened people I know continue to struggle in small and big ways, because they've held on to a story that is saturated with hurt, the need for certainty, and the need for control—which simply doesn't allow them to be the fractal of God they could be. And when they stay stuck, this hurts all of humanity . . . because, as we all know on a cellular level, each of us is connected in an unbreakable chain of love and possibility.

Our vast universe has given us a promise: *the energy of light is always something you can tap into, because it is who you are.* As long as you remember that, it doesn't matter how far you've strayed, how many potholes you've hit along the way, or how treacherous the roads on which you find yourself might be. The light is always waiting for you. And in an instant, like Dorothy tapping her ruby slippers together, it can bring you back home.

I'm largely known as a "manifestation" teacher, but the truth I've come to realize is that nobody wants the *thing* itself. We don't want the house, the soulmate, or even the purposeful job that allows us to be of service—rather, what we're searching for is the *emotional* experience that each of these experiences will give us. We want the experience of freedom and the full panorama of life in all its beauty and diversity. And if this is what we want, we have to start accessing the unbridled wisdom of the heart, which is a powerful interface between the human and the divine, between the shadows of ignorance and the light of ultimate truth.

I want you to know that I don't merely "believe" you can experience deep fulfillment and joy when you tap into the light: I know this to be the unequivocal truth. I see miracles of awareness that happen on a daily basis when people widen the aperture of their perception and embrace the light within.

And guess what? This requires bringing all parts of you to the party, not just the ones your human story (more on this later) likes—sorry! You'll see as you read *The Promise* how important your tender human parts are to the gigantic tapestry of the divine story. The divine story is pure light, and it's inviting you on this amazing soulful adventure. There's so much to experience—but hold in mind that even if the process you'll experience in this book twists your preexisting ideas around a bit, this journey is meant to be fun and enlightening. It'll probably also feel at least a *little* familiar to you—after all, you are part of the light, even if you sometimes forget.

Light is where our fundamental essence lives and teaching you how to access it is at the heart of this book.

All of us are like the universe, constantly expanding in multiple directions. As we harness the light, we start to tell a different story about existence. We begin to meet more versions of ourselves—versions that are not stuck in patterns of hopelessness and struggle but are capable of taking flight into new possibilities and new dimensions of experience.

*The Promise* isn't about creating a false divide between "human" and "divine." The divine is the light that lives at the center of *everything*, so it doesn't ask us to disassociate from our human thoughts and feelings. Instead, it helps us step out of the darkness of our limited thinking and into greater acceptance and radical inclusivity of ourselves. *Of all that we are.* This is how we start to envision lives bigger than anything we'd ever previously imagined, just as I did so many years ago when I found the proverbial light at the end of the tunnel. As I discovered, the divine light helps us access the energy of limitlessness and empowerment, which allows us to have the utmost compassion for our personal struggles while also igniting our creative potential.

How can that not feel radically amazing?

## YOUR PATHWAYS TO DIVINE LIGHT

In this book I will share seven pathways inherent to our understanding of how we can step out of the darkness of our human conditioning and find the light that has always been there . . . patiently waiting to guide us back home to the divine. They are:

- Expansion
- Self-Knowledge
- Empathy
- Clarity
- Transmutation
- Co-creation
- Coherence

Every time you feel confused, heartbroken, or stressed, or if you find yourself saying things like, "I'll never be enough," and "I'll never get to experience [fill in the blank with your highest aspiration for your soul]"—let this book be a reminder that you're not alone. Let the seven pathways be the road map that leads you back to the extraordinary truth of who you are: a being of light who maybe lost their way for a moment—which, funnily enough, is a part of the process. Working with these pathways is kind of like zooming out on a map so you can see every aspect of the glorious terrain that surrounds you—or like turning on the lights in a dark house so you can realize, "Oh, that's what I was bumping into! And look at all the other beautiful stuff I couldn't see!"

I've witnessed the pathways at work in my life, and in the lives of millions of people whom I've helped steward into their own divine story. So I know that with these principles, you'll cultivate awareness of and devotion to your inner light, however your soul wishes for it to manifest and for you to find it. Perfection isn't the goal here—and there may be times when the love, wonder, and magic you experience will come in the aftermath of loss, heartbreak, or just plain numbness. But I will also tell you this: miracles and synchronicities will grace your journey.

Throughout this process, my hope is that you'll feel me right beside you, holding your hand, laughing and crying with you, and gently challenging you to see through a new perspective and question the one you've taken for granted . . . the one that leaves you frustrated, stuck, and bogged down in your perceived inadequacies and limitations.

Each chapter focuses on a different pathway and includes a series of reflection questions as well as a longer practice that is meant to reconnect you with the light within. Please—and I can't emphasize this enough—remember to stop and do self-care as you dive into these questions and practices. The process will feel safer for you if you can approach it with love in your heart. Love is the lubricant of light, and you will find that you can access more information within yourself when love (or even just the intention to invite it in) is present.

## MY WAY HOME TO THE LIGHT

I found the light when I was 25 years old. Or, maybe it would be more accurate to say that the light found me.

After years of toxicity—filled with terrible choices, abusive partners, emotional pain, and anxiety and loneliness that hung over me like a heavy cloud—I finally surrendered. I threw in the towel, at last, on my attempts to handle my life with the same old tools I'd previously used to no effect. I now understand that those tools were dull, broken, and woefully, poignantly human.

But *surrender*? It was divine. That particular night, as I fell to my knees feeling both despair and hope, I experienced a truly authentic and honest release. I was in no way "perfect" and my journey was far from over, but at that moment there was an ease within me I'd never felt before.

I chose myself . . . my true self . . . my divine self, who was deeply committed to a life of serving humanity, no matter how flawed and desperate the previous chapters of my brief existence had been. I was willing to let go of all the coping mechanisms I had quietly, unconsciously used to white-knuckle and control my way through life. I was ready to let go of the emotional and spiritual armor that had made me so impenetrable that the light had never totally been able to get through. In dropping the person I thought I was, I embraced my essence. I felt vast, uncontainable. I saw the light enough to realize I *was* the light.

I was clueless as to what would happen next—how I could embrace and sustain the changes I so badly wanted to make, or even what the steps to change were. Heck, I was unclear on what the next day would look like! It didn't matter, though. As I sat there, sobbing and gently rocking myself, I just knew I would be okay, even if the future was unknown. The purity of that experience carried me through, and my life began to rapidly take new shape.

I left an unhealthy relationship, as well as the financial security of my job, and I began the journey of stepping away from everything that had ever felt unsupportive and that had caused me to be inauthentic. Because I was drastic and radical in my approach, the changes came accordingly, and the positive effects were just as radical. Almost magically, the right kinds of people began showing up to support me, to love me fully, and to remind me of my light without any fear that I would abandon or outshine them if I were to fully step into my authentic self.

I was finally leaning into the divine and relying on it for full support—something I hadn't done since I was a child.

I want to show you that your journey toward finding the light—unique to you but common to all human beings—doesn't need to be filled with blood, sweat, toil, and heartbreak. As the saying goes, on this roller-coaster ride called life, pain is inevitable, but suffering is optional. And that, dear reader, is what this book is all about.

## COMING BACK TO SOURCE ENERGY

Throughout history, we've been faced with the darkness of the human condition—and we've also had glimmers of light in the form of teachers and philosophies that showed us there was a different way to live . . . one that allowed us to experience greater harmony and peace, even as we navigated the ups and downs of being divine beings in finite form. This is our divine story.

Today, we witness a global situation that mirrors back to us the messes that have not been collectively resolved; it's also plain to see in the stories that cause us to feel powerless, panicked, out of control, and disconnected from ourselves and each other. Many of us are flailing in a sea of personal and interpersonal discord, but if we learned to direct our consciousness differently . . . to connect to a much larger story than the soul-deadening myth into which we've written ourselves . . . we could change everything in our internal and external reality.

We all need specific lessons during different times in our lives, and my hope is that this book offers a simple but profound touchstone that will meet you where you're at and give you precisely what you need to return "home." You don't need to make a bunch of changes all at once or institute multiple rituals in order to give yourself a spiritual leg up. In fact, realigning with your spiritual nature can be surprisingly simple. I am not saying it doesn't require some elbow grease, but the perception of effort is much different when leaned into with high-vibration energy and not just willpower, as I'll show you throughout this book. In fact, it was always meant to be!

The tools I'm offering you are the ones that helped me shift my life permanently and to know without a doubt that more was available. To date, I've helped three million beautiful souls worldwide use these tools to access the same sense of freedom, hope, and possibility that I experienced after that moment of surrender. I know this healing is available to absolutely everyone, no matter what their human story has looked like up until now.

Whether you're feeling a little lost and confused, or you've lived large parts of your human story inside the frequency of darkness and intense trauma, this journey through the seven pathways will help you reclaim your access to the light.

Are you ready? Don't worry if your palms are sweaty and your heart is going pitter-patter—that just means you're alive! I'll be your spiritual flashlight, and my energy will be there with you every step of the way to remind you that you've got this!

# CHAPTER 1

# expansion

**Expansion**, the first pathway of light, invites us to shift out of our human story to embrace the light within. Going within, paradoxically, invites us to see the bigger picture and to recognize that it is so much bigger than we ever understood. We start to become more comfortable navigating the unknown. We start to see that life is an awe-inspiring mystery, and there is so much more to it than we might initially perceive.

One of my deepest experiences of expansion occurred in one of my darkest moments, after I went through a miscarriage. When I and my husband Oliver were ready for another baby, as soon as we fell into that readiness, it happened—we were pregnant just a few weeks later. I loved that we had a beautiful family already—two amazing sons who were my heart. But I had the sense that we would have a daughter who would round out our beautiful family. This vision of what our family could be—a little girl who would be protected by her older brothers, with two parents who adored all of them—seemed like it was about to be fulfilled. My pregnancy was easeful. On top of that, I was about to launch my book *8 Secrets to Powerful Manifesting* and things were moving right along. My life looked ideal on paper and in reality . . . and that's when things took a sharp turn.

About 11 or 12 weeks into the pregnancy, I got an ultrasound . . . and was informed that the baby didn't have a heartbeat. My daughter, whom we'd already named Eliana, had passed away, although there were no signs of a miscarriage, such as bleeding or pain. When I look back on that time, I can see I was in a state of severe shock, but what a blessing it was to have three women, two ob-gyns and one midwife, comforting me in such a tangible way. I felt so supported to be in a room with these angelic souls, who all held me as I received the news that no mother-to-be wants to hear. It was only when I got home that I miscarried physically. It was as if I were being cradled in a gentle process, so I could learn about the loss while surrounded in love and support. It was an oddly beautiful experience, as I went through a full spectrum of emotions that I allowed myself to express rather than suppress. I felt like I was experiencing the entire cycle of life and death, and it was overwhelming but deeply moving.

It was a nonlinear process. Both Oliver and I went through a period that alternated between joy and grief, acceptance and rage. There was some part of us that couldn't understand why this was happening. However, this is where my awareness of the light saved me. I refused to stay in tunnel vision. I continued to express my very human pain while recognizing that there was so much more to the story than what I was currently telling myself. I sought the kind of clarity that would help me to understand what was happening in a larger, deeper way—one that would help me to meet the somber beauty of loss and expand into my divine self.

Of course, my ego continued to contract and react to this pain by asking, "How on earth did I manifest *this*?" But amid those waves of grief, I kept going back to a place of genuine gratitude and the desire to understand what was emerging. One of my dearest friends, Tracy, told me, "I know I can say this to you, and I know you can receive it: this was the greatest act of unconditional love there could be."

Everything became so clear from that moment. I understood what Tracy meant. I could see my daughter, Eliana, in the beautiful, high, light vibration that was her essence. As painful as it was to be a mother burying her own child before getting a chance to really know her, I had Tracy helping me to see that Eliana had given me a powerful gift by reminding me of where I come from and where I will eventually return. It was an experience of exquisite surrender because it helped me to understand that this was not merely a "loss," not merely something to mourn.

I was a mother who'd lost her daughter, but expanding into the light equipped me with what I needed to handle such a dark situation and to recognize it as a part of my personal purpose. This wasn't me spiritually bypassing my way to an easier place (because I won't lie—it was hard!), but I came to understand that Eliana was here for the amount of time she was meant to be, and with her she'd brought a beautiful frequency of love and light that pointed to the next level into which our family was growing. This was what Tracy meant when she spoke about the act of unconditional love that this gorgeous soul had gone through, just for us. Eliana was taking us somewhere far more vast and beautiful than the place we'd been living (which was already pretty wonderful, but the divine light is all about expansion!). She had come straight from source to deliver this lesson in the only way she could—to show us the frequency she was clearly pointing us toward, and to give us the free will to do what we choose. We were being invited to expand—to raise our vibration to the extent that we just couldn't drop back down into the level where we previously existed. Instead, we started to invite people into the new place we'd come into.

What I began to see was that I wasn't just a grieving mother with so many lost hopes and desires. And Eliana wasn't just my daughter. "Mother" and "daughter" were just human roles that hid the true nature of our relationship. I knew that this was a soul-to-soul, source-energy-to-source-energy connection that existed in divine light. And because Eliana gave me a glimpse of that, what I received was utterly sublime. I peeked behind the curtain of the human story and into the light that pervades the space of the divine story. It broke my heart open.

I'd been a frequent visitor to rock bottom in the past, but this wasn't that. It was like I'd been sitting in the dark, and then someone turned a light on—and when I looked around, all I saw was beauty.

Even a simple shift of perspective from a much less dramatic experience can offer a magnificent example of shifting into the divine story, where the light lives. Every time I've done this, I've gone through a rebirthing process that ultimately led me to the life I have now—one in which there's even more beauty, magic, love, and success (albeit, a very different definition of success than my previous one) than I could ever have imagined. There is no possible way my mind could have conjured up, let alone believed, I'd be where I am today.

It was also my way of deeply receiving and accepting a new kind of story—what was possible when I was willing to surrender to the vast scope of the divine . . . to *expand into* a light that was much brighter than I used to be comfortable with.

## A SIMPLE QUESTION

Expansion—being able to expand out of the shadows and into the light—is the first and most fundamental pathway. For too many people, the experience of suffering can overwhelm us with feelings of unworthiness and shame—as if we need to change everything in our lives in order to be "good," or "spiritual." Even when we know we're spiraling into disastrous thought processes or reliving old traumas, we don't know how to get out of that state. I assure you that the Promise of the divine is that *we are never not whole*, even in the times we feel sorely lacking. We don't have to dramatically clean out every negative thought, belief, action, or behavior. In truth, all we need to do is get curious, which is the first step to expanding our perspective and stepping into a higher, lighter vibration.

Again, living in the light is not about perfectionism or "getting it right." The divine never intended for us to struggle or be perfect to find a way home. Struggle is a perception of reality we can throw new lenses on. In truth, all we need to do is ask ourselves a simple question to begin the process of expansion, which is the basis of everything you're going to read in this book: *Am I living in the darkness, or am I reaching toward the light?*

Your answer will be "darkness" if you find yourself falling into some of the patterns that are common to most people. These patterns can sometimes escape our notice (hence the reason they tend to hang out in the "shadows"), so I've included them below. We most commonly experience these states when everything in life feels like an uphill battle, we don't feel that we're living a life aligned with our highest ideals, and we don't wake up with the emotional experience we want or have the tools to create it. Don't despair if you relate to any of what I've listed below! It's just a sign that it's high time to expand into the light.

## YOUR "STORY" IS FOCUSED ON THE EXTERNAL, NOT THE INTERNAL

Be forewarned—a huge aspect of the process of shifting into the light is introspection. A little bit of inquiry goes a long way, and it all starts with the way you talk to yourself and others about who you are and where you've been.

If I asked you to tell me about your life and your story up till now, how might you answer? You can garner a lot of information about someone based on how they respond to such a question.

For example, if somebody focuses on everything that's going wrong ("I was in a tumultuous relationship and I have two children who got taken away, and I have no idea where I'm going next"), this is a clear indication that they're deep in the darkness of their human story. The details they offer are external in that they focus on events, people, and situations outside of them. They have also chosen to define the glorious, messy, complex terrain of who they are on the basis of past experiences. For them, life is a series of data points, occurrences, and experiences that have little to nothing to do with their inner truth. They usually lack introspection or insight. In many cases, they define themselves on the basis of their specific roles—who they are in relation to the world ("I'm a CEO and a mom and a wife, and I love playing tennis").

There's nothing wrong with any of these identifications; at times, it makes sense to define yourself in this way. But these labels don't really get to the core of who a person is; they tend to fixate on temporary identities and experiences. When I ask people about their story, what I *really* want to know is who they are, what their purpose is, what makes them light up! These are the aspects of our deeper truth that we often gloss over. (I'm seriously hoping that the perennial dinner-table question, "What do you do for a living?" gets replaced once and for all by something like, "What makes you come alive?")

When someone uses internal reference points—their values, longings, and convictions—to answer a question like "Who are you?" it's pretty obvious that they're going way down to the root and essence of their being—that this is the way they define their life and their sense of self. They are living in their divine light—maybe not in every moment of every day, which isn't even necessary, but more often than not. It is our external reference points— the job we work at, the amount of money we make, the roles we've taken on, the events that have been milestones in our lives—that are the benchmarks of our human story. Again, some of these aspects can be wonderful and enriching, but if you were to wake up tomorrow and all of these things were gone, who would you be? How would you feel? It is only when the human story is connected to the light within that we find ourselves greeting life as an adventure rather than something to endure.

## Reflection Questions

1. If I asked you to tell me about your life in five minutes, what would you say? How would you define yourself?

2. How focused is your story of your life on external things (what you do for a living; identities you hold, such as mother or CEO; things from your past that continue to impact you, etc.)?

3. How focused is your story of your life on your internal process (major life lessons and themes that have helped you to grow, your sense of purpose, your awareness of your feelings and emotional state, etc.)?

## YOU FEEL LIKE A VICTIM OF CIRCUMSTANCE

Another indicator that we're operating solely from our human story is when we feel like a victim of circumstance—like the world is against us and we need to do our best to stay vigilant. I certainly felt justified in living in victimhood for a good portion of my own life. Sometimes vigilance doesn't work, and a person might collapse into hopelessness and despair. They're beleaguered by a "why me?" mentality in which they're always the sad protagonist in a story of star-crossed fates.

When I talk about the victim mentality, I want to stress that people have every right to feel like victims from time to time—so please don't confuse this concept with victim blaming. I myself have had horrific things happen to me, and I constantly meet people who have lived through the worst atrocities. When such people share their stories with me, I don't tell them that they need to give up their victim positions—that would be callous, and to an extent untrue (since it's very important for us to be able to feel and acknowledge our pain and the points in our lives when our boundaries have been violated). However, when people get stuck in this story, it can be a prison with no exits—one that impacts not just them, but also the people they know, and potentially, their entire life quality and experience.

While it's absolutely possible for people to heal from such experiences, and to use them as a launchpad for helping others, not everyone decides to take a path of healing. For example, I know a woman who has experienced extreme sexual trauma in her life. Sadly, she suffers from a few mental disorders, due to these and other experiences.

Ever heard the saying that "hurt people hurt people"? This encapsulates the reason so many people who have been victimized and harmed can end up becoming perpetrators. That was unfortunately true of this woman too. In many ways, she would use her victim status to lure people in and to then take advantage of and abuse them in turn. But in her mind, she wasn't doing anything wrong. If anyone called her out on this, she would simply default to, "I'm the victim here. I was abused as a child." Her suffering was the distorted lens through which she saw everything around her, but she didn't realize she'd turned this into an upside-down power that she used to manipulate others and avoid taking accountability for her own bad behavior. I could see this was not the highest way for her to go about her life, as it led to her jumping in and out of dysfunctional relationships, hurting her children, and of course, hurting herself. The light of her beautiful soul was in there, but her human story wouldn't let it come out very often.

When we feel like a victim in every part of our lives, this becomes a blind spot that dominates our decisions. Victim mentality can make a person extremely self-involved, in the same way a small child thinks the entire world revolves around them. But this is the tragedy of the unhealed parts of ourselves when they begin to dominate the rest of our lives. If someone has fallen into victimhood, they've found a way to get their basic needs of connection, love, and acceptance met—certainly, it's not the healthiest way to live, but it can serve to validate that something terrible happened in the past and keep the person from moving into a more mature and holistic way of making sense of it (e.g., "The pain I went through has helped me to understand the power of forgiveness—especially self-forgiveness—for the decisions I made when I was in survival mode"). Very few people *consciously* choose to stay stuck—which is exactly why moving into the light necessitates an honest and loving assessment of how victimhood has kept you from knowing your wholeness.

Just like everyone else, I've had my own baptisms by fire, and there were times when I'd throw up my hands and exclaim, "This is just the way I am, take it or leave it!" I wasn't ready to assume responsibility for my erratic behavior or my dismal circumstances. After all, I didn't see that I'd created it, but that I was a by-product of it. I had to shift into an empowered version of myself, and the only way I could do that was to examine my victimhood without judgment.

Again, I want to reiterate that if you have been a victim of abuse, like so many people I've met (and myself), it's not your fault. You didn't manifest it. You didn't deserve it. At the same time, you are not what you experienced—and you can make the powerful choice to transmute the pain and suffering so that you don't have to live out a version of that story for the rest of your life. What happened to you isn't your fault, but it is your responsibility to learn how to deal with what has been placed on your path. As Chapter 5: Transmutation will share in greater detail, it's even possible to locate your greatest gifts within that pain. But to do that, you have to remember that within you is a vast and capable being; and during the times you didn't feel its presence, it was merely lying dormant, waiting for you to expand into your light.

**Reflection Questions**

1. In what ways are you stuck in a story of yourself as a victim? Dig deep here, as your victimhood may also mask itself with "toughness."

2. How does this story keep you from being accountable to yourself and others?

3. What are the lingering fears that keep you from being truly empowered and living your best life?

## YOU SELF-SABOTAGE BECAUSE
## YOU'RE AFRAID OF BEING HAPPY

Another sign that you're stuck in your human story is that, no matter how much you want something that is part of your innate light (love, peace, abundance, connection to your purpose), you can't seem to have it. This isn't because you aren't capable of achieving the life of your dreams; it's because there's some covert part of you that is self-sabotaging because it misunderstands what it means to be truly fulfilled. For example, this part of you might not feel deserving of happiness, or maybe it can't even imagine what it would look or feel like. Sometimes, we settle for less not because we are afraid we won't achieve it, but because we know we *will*, and the fears that come from the idea of stepping more fully into our power can hold us back just as greatly. In many cases, self-sabotage occurs because the prospect of what we might have to give up to experience living in our divine light feels too difficult or even impossible.

As Marianne Williamson famously said, "Our deepest fear is not that we are inadequate. Our deepest fear is that we are powerful beyond measure. It is our light, not our darkness, that most frightens us." I had a wake-up call around the possibility of shining my light brightly during a meditation when I interrogated myself about the worst thing that could happen if I got everything I wanted, including financial abundance.

What people often don't recognize is that we're always in the process of manifesting our reality. I call it "countermanifestation" when we create results we don't want because we're not aware of the conversation we're having with the universe. Our conscious mind is shooting off in one direction into the quantum field, saying, "Yes, I want this!" but the subconscious says, "Pump the brakes! It's not safe! Bad things can happen! You're not worthy!"

I had the sense, even back then, that something was amiss in the way I was relating to my desires. I wanted to understand the true conversation I was having with the universe, aka myself. I wanted to know why I was asking for things that caused me pain. I intuited that some part of me—the part of me that was currently operating the most strongly in my psyche—was scared to death. If it hadn't been, I would be moving toward abundance without any qualms about it. My energy would be whole and potent as I ran through the quantum field creating the reality I consciously most wanted. As I sat in contemplation, things began to get more and more clear. And that's when the truth crept up on me—that my interpretation of the past was sabotaging my ability to be happy in the present.

It's not always easy to recognize self-sabotage when you're the one doing it, but you've probably noticed it in other people. I have a close girlfriend, Rhonda, who is a vibrant woman in her 70s. Rhonda had tragically lost her husband in a plane crash, but she was attempting to move on with her life. I visited her several years ago, when she was in a turbulent relationship with a much younger man who lived in a different country. While some of her other friends questioned her choices, I'd simply said, "Go for it if it really makes you happy." However, as Rhonda and I spent more time together, it was clear to me that her relationship wasn't good for her soul. When he was around, her boyfriend swept her off her feet with grand gestures; however, he'd then disappear for long periods of time without any communication. Rhonda was constantly on a pendulum swing between giddy love and abject misery.

21

"Rhonda, is this what you really want?" I gently asked her.

She shook her head. "Of course not! It's painful. I want a love that's consistent, something I can count on."

I shook my head. "No, you don't."

Rhonda furrowed her brow. "What do you mean?"

"Please just go with me, Rhonda. I'm sorry if this triggers you. But you lost your husband in such an abrupt way. Don't you think this relationship you're in mirrors that loss? Some part of you is comfortable having chaotic energy around you. Maybe it's so you won't be surprised or hurt if your boyfriend actually leaves. This way, there's a kind of 'safety' in that you're always prepared to lose him."

Rhonda began bawling. Something had clicked within her and interrupted the pattern, stripping it of its power. From that moment on, she was able to make better decisions and to be conscious of how her fear had been inadvertently guiding her life. But it was only because she was willing to sit with and observe her own pain, instead of running away from it, that she could release herself from the ball and chain of behaviors that were not serving her.

Self-sabotage can occur when we're afraid of directly confronting our pain. We fear what we might find, and how it will make us feel. But for both Rhonda and me, allowing ourselves to fully sit with the pain of the patterns that prevailed in our lives, and that kept us from a more fulfilling relationship with abundance or love, actually opened us up to more truth. Because we were no longer running away from the situation or placing Band-Aids over it, we could simply be with it. We didn't have to struggle for another few decades, wondering why things were going wrong. Instead, we'd found a way to conquer the issue in a short period of time—simply by being real.

One thing to remember about self-sabotage is that it's typically based on unconscious rules we've created for ourselves. Rhonda's rule looked something like: love is inherently unstable. Clearly, this was based on her experience of losing her husband. The energetic stamp of her trauma left her with a new wiring that was attempting to heal that trauma, albeit incorrectly. That's why she opted for the whirlwind romance, which perfectly aligned with her rule, even if it brought little in the way of true fulfillment. It wasn't until Rhonda was able to locate a stable foundation of love within herself that she began to attract healthy, communicative romantic relationships.

Our human story is limited in that it makes up stories about our past to protect us from our future. Similar to the subconscious reel I write about in *8 Secrets to Powerful Manifesting*, it tries to keep us "safe" by limiting our options, but this never really works—because our soul longs to stretch out into the vastness and grandeur of life itself, not stay stuck within the confines of the familiar.

Our divine light helps us to see that our rules can be arbitrary and untrue. The divine is all about breaking human rules and showing us that even if we didn't know it before, it truly is possible to have it all. Now, the perception of "having it all" will vastly differ for each person, and even depending on the phase you're in, so you may not even know what true fulfillment looks like in your 3D world just yet. Even if you don't know what the solution is off the top of your head, that's okay. Sitting with your pain with patience and compassion rather than fear and avoidance automatically creates a window into new possibilities and even bends time—often taking us through the discomfort of these moments at warp speed.

## Reflection Questions

1.  What are the "rules" you have created that are getting in the way of you being totally fulfilled? Remember, a rule is there to ensure that a belief is maintained, even if that belief is faulty, so it may be helpful to first assess your environment and ask yourself, *What beliefs do I most likely have, based on how my relationships/self-image/ financial situation, etc., are right now?* Then you can work your way backward.

2.  What do you fear is the worst that can happen if you get what you want?

3.  What past event or pattern is continuing to play out in your life when you believe that story is valid?

4.  What belief do you need to develop now to accept that you truly *can* have it all?

## YOU THINK YOU'RE BROKEN BEYOND REPAIR

Another indication that you're living in your human story is that you've embraced a sad narrative that sounds a lot like, "I've messed up too much to deserve anything beautiful. I'm not good enough. Because of everything that's happened to me, I'm broken."

No one is broken. It's a disempowering thought, and truly false. I've never met anyone whom I can't see the perfection in (and I've served people from many walks of life). That belief has never wavered within me. I understand why people hold on to the perception of brokenness.

I did too. It's another example of how we use the past, and our incomplete interpretations of what has happened to us, as an excuse to stay stuck. Because even if we're miserable, sometimes the familiarity of our misery is the only solace we can seem to find.

Often, this idea that a person is broken comes from the tendency to take one fragmented aspect of the self and see it as the whole picture (something we'll be getting a lot more into in Chapter 2: Self-Knowledge). This can occur when one energetically powerful (and usually traumatic) moment in time is chosen to define oneself. This is a typical reaction to trauma, as the brain now begins to build protective mechanisms to ensure that trauma is never experienced again—but there always comes a point in our journey when our self-protective measures become obsolete and even harmful. This also occurs when we take a small fragment of another person—let's say, their confidence—and use it to define them. But the truth is, we can never know someone else's full story based on a snapshot!

Comparison envy is a false way of assessing our own perceived progress or worth. It's natural to compare ourselves to people who seem to have made it or figured things out, but the reason this doesn't work is that a fragmented, unhealed part of us is the one that's perceiving or trying to figure out how it can achieve greatness or happiness. We've got it all backward. We can't see our divine self through a human lens. Too often, we find ourselves looking for perfection, but that's not the same thing as wholeness. We can use our admiration for others to help ourselves expand instead of getting squashed by the envy that keeps us stuck and separate, fumbling around in the darkness.

This is why I like to share my messy and glorious background with other people, since so many of us tend to judge based on what the surface looks like. But in all honesty, if you had met me 15 years ago, I can promise I was spiritually way further behind than anyone can imagine. So, I have total compassion for people who struggle with not feeling good enough, or who believe that for them to be happy, they need to become a totally different person with a totally different past from the one they have.

For so many of us, the experience of suffering can be overwhelming—we've forgotten who we are: divine beings having a human experience.

I struggled with this a lot prior to jumping into the world of spirituality and personal development. I always had the deep desire to help others, but I felt unworthy. I would ask myself, "Who am I to do this?" I had so many rules around how spiritual a person I needed to be to bring light into anyone else's life—and what those so-called spiritual qualities were. When it came down to it, I felt that I had to be Mother Teresa—completely untouched by any form of "sin." But this idea that I needed to be perfect didn't even allow me to get started!

If I hadn't stepped into who I am today, I can't imagine how many people I would have failed to help. And I didn't help those people by magically becoming my human story's version of a godly, spiritual person. (And let's face it—it's pretty obvious when someone's faking it!) I became the person committed to service by surrendering to the divine light within—which doesn't have a whole lot of rules about worthiness or perfection, or any of that stuff! I learned that we naturally move toward goodness, toward love, toward service, because these are a part of our essence. The seemingly terrible, selfish, unspiritual things we did or experienced in the past were just tactics we learned to protect ourselves or to cope in our lost moments. Once we know better, we must do better, but we will never allow ourselves to step into the "better" aspect if we don't change the lens through which we see ourselves.

The rules we have about who we need to be in order to be successful, happy, of service, fill-in-the-blank-with-your-desired-goal—ensure that we miss out on contributing what is uniquely ours to give to the world: our perfect puzzle piece, if you will. So many of us are walking around trying to jam ourselves into a corner when we're meant to be somewhere in the middle. Through the divine lens, it is our "mistakes" and understanding that help us to shift into humility, forgiveness, and a broader perspective. And this is how we come to meet the most beautiful version of ourselves.

So, I'm here to remind you that in every moment you feel broken and unfulfilled, you have the capacity to shift into the light and embrace your wholeness—and best of all, you don't have to give up your experience of pain and suffering, or talk yourself into feeling differently.

Remembering your essential wholeness can help you to expand. All you have to do is remember that your true identity is much more vast than this moment in time. This can help you to transmute any resistance, shift you out of tunnel vision, and immediately connect you to source energy—to the light within.

The Austrian psychiatrist Viktor Frankl, who developed a school of psychotherapy known as *logotherapy* (which asserts that our search for meaning is central to the human experience), was a Holocaust survivor whose inspiring story entailed finding a sense of freedom, meaning, and hope while he was a prisoner in several concentration camps. His story is a prime example of the fact that there is a divine and unbreakable core of courage, wisdom, and light that lives within every single person. And, as extreme as it may sound, no matter what we are subjected to, this aspect of the self is always there, and it is always available to help us heal so that we can live meaningful, purposeful lives. People like Frankl didn't allow the depths and darkness of human experience to consume them; rather, they allowed these things to become their motivation to thrive and to change the human story on this planet.

But none of that can happen without you recognizing you're never, *ever* broken. (Also, ever heard that Rumi line, "The wound is where the light enters"?)

At this point, you might be saying, "That sounds really nice, Mandy, but honestly? I *feel* broken! I can't just hit an off button." Trust me, I get it! Have you ever experienced the annoyance that comes from someone telling you to "just cheer up" when you're down in the dumps? I have, and it sucks!

The great thing is, the divine is built into our DNA. There is no point at which we are not whole; it's just that we've forgotten what that feels like. We got so busy looking left that we forgot the divine was smiling at us a head turn to the right. If you don't remember what it's like to feel whole in the moment, don't worry—it really is possible to work your way back into a lighter vibration. Just because you're sitting in anger or hopelessness right now doesn't mean you can't get a taste of that wholeness again. It can be as simple as contemplating the last time you were truly happy, and then allowing yourself to be available to the sensations and emotions associated with that experience. It could be leaning on a little faith in the truth I'm sharing here and believing what I believe: that the best is right around the corner, but it's up to you to round the bend.

Most of all, remember that the human story is actually part of the divine light, but it's just one piece of it. We're here on this wild ride through conflict and heartache and sorrow and ecstasy for a reason, and it's not to wallow. It's to remember what Dr. Frankl realized in his darkest hour: Every single one of us is worthy and whole, no matter what we've done or what we've experienced. And since the divine doesn't work in human time, it's possible to remember this in a split second.

## Reflection Questions

1. In what ways do you feel "broken" or unworthy of living your highest potential? How does this impact your life on a day-to-day basis?

2. Whose voice is holding you back? (For example, it might be the voice of a critical parent or an abusive boss.)

3. What are your rules around who you need to be in order to be loved or to live a meaningful life in which you get to contribute to the greater good? It may be helpful to think back to your childhood and ask yourself: *Who did I have to be in order to be loved/not hurt?*

4. Is there a time in your life when you felt truly whole? (Extra credit if you invite the sensations and emotions associated with that experience into your present moment.) It's okay if you can't recall a time—it just shows how deep inside the human story you might be. I can't wait to lovingly continue helping you pull yourself out and gently redirect you toward the light.

## YOU'RE LIVING FROM YOUR MIND, NOT YOUR HEART

There are a lot of indications that will alert you to the fact that you're living in your human story rather than your divine one, and while I've only enumerated the big ones for the sake of simplicity, this final one is probably *the* biggest of all. When you live in your human story, you're stuck in your thoughts—the constructs we've created in order to get from point A to point B. But most of the time, they're the constructs we've created to feel safe, or to assure ourselves that life is predictable and we can indeed have absolute control over everything.

Yeah, right!

The divine story, in contrast, is one in which the heart leads. The open heart doesn't need to have control, because it's in *charge* and it recognizes that while the human realm may not always be "safe," putting our trust in the power of love and the transcendent light of the divine will always take us where we need to go with a greater feeling of support than we ever believed possible.

This is a tricky one for people to grok. There are so many incredible, curious, kind, and passionate souls who long to share their gifts with the world—and who've tried and failed to "think" their way into happiness. Most people I work with are women ages 35 to 65, from every walk of life, who want to be self-actualized and to lead soulfully driven lives. But the biggest thing that stops them from getting there is the tendency to intellectualize spiritual information, to jam-pack their tired and hardworking brains with that information instead of processing it through the heart. It's a lot like knowing a language but having no idea how to actually speak it. This is why my work includes a mixture of science and psychology—I want to appease my left-brainers. Honestly, the magic happens when we placate the mind so it can finally chill out and let the heart do its thing!

There's nothing wrong with the intellect, but the light doesn't live in the brain alone; it lives in the body and in the heart, which is the metaphorical and literal instrument of love. So, we can go to as many spiritual workshops and retreats as we want, and we can even start to sound like we're walking our talk in tangible ways—but if we haven't processed any of this stuff through the heart, it ain't gonna show up!

In my past, I've sat with some of the most intelligent people on this planet, who held vast amounts of information about psychology, quantum physics, and how the brain is wired. Sharing space with them didn't make me feel very smart until I actually learned how to utilize and connect all that information in practical ways—which is at the basis of all my work. These intellects referred to me as "the bridge" because I could take what they shared and use it to help others from varying walks of life. Instead of demeaning the work I did, they acknowledged that it was important to have me in the room because, according to them, my heart and presence kept the environments open and expansive.

The human story is all about accumulating more knowledge in the form of ideas, but the divine light transcends ideas. It's about deep feeling and embodiment. Yes, energy is entering the body through our endocrine glands, and we're interpreting it and responding to it through our neurology, but the actual process is happening without any need for scientific understanding.

We are all embodied beings, and we get on some level that the heart trumps the intellect. When we meet someone who is out of alignment, we can sense that something is off without needing to "understand" why. And when we meet someone who immediately puts us at ease, we can recognize that they're embodying their light in a particular way that goes beyond knowledge in the form of facts and ideas—it's more about *knowing* in every cell of the body. (Which is why spiritual transmissions that are crystallized as knowledge only get at a tiny fraction of the teacher's intended meaning.)

The head-to-heart connection is very important. But we walk around in our heads because we've been taught that the pain we're so actively trying to avoid lives in our hearts. In truth, the head can be a very dangerous place to live if we're there 24/7! It's full of worst-case scenarios and attacks from inner critics. When we start to become receptive to the wisdom of the heart, we start to open up to our innate wisdom, strength, power, and dignity. We start to relocate the wholeness that we've been searching for, albeit unconsciously, and we realize that it's always been within us, waiting to share its love and light.

### Reflection Questions

1.  In what ways have you been living from your mind rather than your heart? (Reflect on this with no self-judgment, which comes from the mind, as you know!)

2.  What are some of the reasons you do this (e.g., you've been hurt in the past, which has made you close your heart off to yourself and others; you've gotten praise for being cerebral,

so that's your comfort zone; you've been conditioned to believe that you need to have a lot of "knowledge" to be worthy, etc.)?

3. Was there a time when you acted from your heart (which is not to be confused with mind-based fears, scarcity mentality, or failing to trust your gut feelings because your ego wanted a specific outcome)? How was that for you?

## SHIFTING INTO THE LIGHT: EMBRACING THE TRUE MEANING OF SURRENDER

So far, you know that a simple question can shift you into the light within, and you've discovered even more questions that can get you there. Now, for the remainder of this chapter, we'll get into the nitty-gritty of how you can begin to shift into the light with even more ease and willingness.

If it isn't obvious already, surrender is the key to living in the light. That can seem like a tall order, because there's a degree of certainty and consistency the human mind requires for us to feel safe. However, sometimes the need for certainty can make us miserable—for example, if we grow comfortable with abusive partners and less-than-stellar work situations, because hey, at least they are familiar!

When we step into surrender, we aren't abdicating our power; instead, we're relaxing so we can enter the flow of what's right in front of us (often, hidden in plain sight) and what's supposed to happen next. I believe there's some form of a divine plan for every single one of us, but too often, we have to hit rock bottom to finally let go. However, I encourage you to surrender *before* you find yourself stumbling around in your own personal basement. If you're willing to even tiptoe through some of your fear of the unknown, I promise you'll discover your own version of heaven on earth—where peace is your frequent companion, where you feel that you are doing what you came here to do, where you are easefully magnetizing the events that make you even more of who you truly are.

When you surrender, you lean into trust. The thing I often say to reluctant people who think playing with surrender is basically the same as leaping off a mountain without a parachute is that they're not putting their life in the hands of some abstract, distant idea. *The divine is us.* When we trust the divine, we trust ourselves. We come to see that we've always been trustworthy and capable, even when our human story was telling us otherwise. We may have been shut off from this energy for so long it feels hard to find, but our divine story light is right in front of us—it's within us.

During the times in my life when I was unhappiest, those where when I was doing my damndest to control my narrative and make it seem like I had it all together. However, I didn't trust myself *at all.* Instead, I stuck to the tried and true, the straight and narrow. I didn't dream big or open my heart to new possibilities, because that could mean I might fail.

When I began trusting myself, I realized the outcome didn't matter one bit. No matter what happened, I now had the awareness that I could be centered and at peace, whatever the scenario. I knew I'd be able to handle conflict and unexpected challenges, because I was choosing to surrender to the divine—to my open heart, to my intuition, to my light—and it would always catch me if I fell. There was a tomorrow version of me that could handle tomorrow, as long as I leaned into the divine light I had forgotten but that hadn't forgotten me.

A lot of people come to the world of spirituality and personal development because they want to have more control over their lives. They want specific outcomes. There's nothing inherently wrong with this, but it can cut us off from an infinite number of realities that are always forming around us. Holographic realities and parallel universes, anyone? What we say we desire becomes the only reality available to us—and sometimes, it's not actually to our benefit. Where we unconsciously or consciously direct our consciousness is what inevitably manifests. This is always predictable, but if we are manifesting from solely human lenses, our outcomes seldom serve us. Our mind, not our heart, comes to dictate our desires. We close ourselves off from the beautiful possibilities.

Ironically, when we're living from the heart, from a place of surrender, we don't actually have that many desires. I always say I couldn't have dreamed up the life I have now, but even with all I have, I don't want for much other than to feel divine presence in all I do. When we lean into the light, we come to appreciate the unfolding process, which includes everything we are learning about ourselves, through the lens of love. We are excited to experience the vastness of this reality, and we stay open to magic.

Surrender is not interested in specific outcomes. It's more interested in welcoming the marvelous flow of reality. It's here to attune us to the magnificent present so we begin to fall back in love with the journey, instead of holding our breath waiting for a good feeling at the end.

It's natural to have specific ideas about what we want. For example, if I'm planning a family trip, I might have some clearly delineated ideas about how I want things to go. Few people are constantly in a state of surrender! At the same time, I know that surrender is necessary when I feel myself white-knuckling and tunnel-visioning in a way that isn't serving me. So, if I find myself in a pickle, that's okay. It probably means I jumped onto a path that isn't actually working for me, or I have something magical to learn about myself to further expand into the light. Surrender brings me back into the present moment in such a way that I'm not trying to orchestrate the outcome—but I am in charge of my energy and reality from the inside out, because I'm choosing the path of least resistance. When it starts to feel heavy, and when I feel like I'm *not* on the path of least resistance, I remind myself of something important: the path that's light and right is the path I want to be on.

Surrender helps us out of the numerous sticky situations that are part of the human story; it expands the teeny-tiny perspective we might have been stuck in, so that now we can see the possibilities that were previously in our blind spot. With surrender comes clarity (more about that in Chapter 4), and with clarity comes a deeper sense of aliveness that helps us know we're on the right track. It actually solves problems more quickly, and it lets us enjoy the ride.

## Reflection Questions

1. What's your general experience of surrender? Do you find it easy or difficult? Why or why not?

2. What are areas of your life where you've struggled for a sense of control? What has that struggle cost you? Has it ever produced the outcome you were hoping for, or has it been a stressful experience?

3. What are the areas where you find yourself white-knuckling through life? How can you allow a greater sense of surrender in those instances? What might be sitting at the root of your need for control? Is there another way to view it?

## WHAT HAPPENS WHEN THE DIVINE FEELS WAY TOO ABSTRACT?

I've taught more people than I can count to shift into their divine light. But I've also recognized that we can sometimes get in our own way when we have an abstract idea of what the "divine" is. A lot of times, our concepts of the divine obstruct the path to actually *feeling* it. I've met people who get frustrated because the divine seems far away and inaccessible—so, just because they can't feel it in the moment, they shut down and think it's unavailable to them.

I empathize with this, the amount of fulfillment I feel today was truly inaccessible to me 15 years ago. Sure, I felt sparks of it in random moments, but I couldn't fully access or even imagine it. That's why I had to be gentle with myself and take the steps that presented themselves in the flow of surrender. Whenever I needed to rest more than anything else, I wasn't getting down on myself, saying, "Mandy, you need to get to your dream life right

now! Make it happen!" I was still in the process of growing and expanding, so I had to give it time. This actually
condensed the time frame; instead of sitting in that space
for months, I could move through the stickiness with love,
meaning it didn't take that long at all!

Shifting into the light is meant to be a gentle process,
and sometimes, part of that process requires building our
capacity for wonderful things to enter. In this sense, all we
have to do is gather the feedback that is coming to us at all
times, in both the difficult and the wonderful moments.
What we do with that feedback takes us to the next step.
The beautiful reality we want to manifest may usher in
a brand-new reality altogether. For example, when I met
my husband, it wasn't like he just plopped right into my
life. He arrived as I started to welcome in a completely
new life, which developed miraculously over time because
I allowed for it to flow as such.

We are always in a state of evolution, so the journey to
accessing our "greatest" self is just that—a journey! Over
time, living in the light will feel like the most natural
thing in the world, and you'll see results quickly—but you
have to allow yourself to be taken on the wild ride that is
your life. That's why you're here! An old friend of mine
who was a monk used to say to me, "The purpose of life is
life, mon!"

So, if you find yourself feeling frustrated or asking,
*What the heck am I even doing?* just pause, breathe, and take
a few steps back. You don't need to define the light or figure
out what it's all about (again, that's a very human way of
looking at the divine!). Trust that you'll continue to learn,
grow, and master your life, as long as you're willing to ear-
nestly and honestly expand yourself rather than thinking
your way into staying stuck. You've got this! In fact, your

human parts will assist you in accessing the divine (for example, a painful experience in the 3D world can help you tap back into your deep love of humanity)—as long as you recognize that the human story is inherently limited when it's disconnected from the light.

My husband, Oliver, and I have a practice around this. Every time the human story starts to consume us, we consciously choose to slow down. We ask ourselves, "How can we come back to simplicity and surrender?" We utilize our soulful compass to get back on track. We identify the soulful needs that lead us back to a state of surrender and help us to shift back into our light so that we can recognize the divine in all things, even times of difficulty.

## Reflection Questions

1.  What are some of the ideas you have about the divine that make it feel difficult to access (e.g., thinking you need to have a full-blown "awakening" experience to know what it is, believing it's only available to "good" or "perfect" people, etc.)?

2.  Think of a situation in your life that has been a source of pain. How can you come back to simplicity and surrender around this situation?

3.  Think back to a time in your life when you felt the presence of the divine—when you didn't have to "think" your way into it. What did that feel like? Can you invite it in, right here and now?

## GET IN TOUCH WITH YOUR SOULFUL NEEDS

Soulful needs are divine needs—deep inner compasses that orient us to who we really are and what our true nature desires to express and emanate in this lifetime. Our soulful needs connect us to our authentic self and the full extent of our energy and vitality. A soulful need can look like creativity, the desire to be of service to others, joy, courageous action, connection—and the list goes on. When we feel like we're off track, we can always utilize our soulful compass to regain a sense of balance and move in the direction that feels best for us. A soulful need helps to create a greater sense of freedom and expansiveness— and when we're stuck in our human story and don't feel "right," it's usually because there is a soulful need somewhere that's been shoved into the darkness.

How do we identify our soulful needs? It's pretty simple— and simplicity is always a part of this process! As I mentioned earlier, we are all fractals of the divine and there is an aspect within each of us that is intrinsically connected to the light. We get in touch with this divine light when we move toward our wholeness. Interestingly, our actions and the things we are attracted to can often uncover our divine, soulful needs. For example, if you tend to be drawn to creative people but get down on yourself for not being "artistic," your soulful need for creativity is not being fully met because you're projecting it onto the people around you. Or perhaps you find yourself in a string of unfulfilling relationships, and you can't figure out why; the deeper soulful need is for connection, but your human story is one of scarcity and of feeling undeserving, so you are unconsciously bringing the wrong people into your life. I can relate to this one—for years, I was in unfulfilling relationships with people who didn't make me feel loved or wanted. As I came to understand, this was part of my pattern of trauma bonding (the connection that someone has to an abusive person in their life, which is usually part of an unhealthy recurring cycle).

There are many ways to bypass our own resistance and to work with the inner conflict that can keep us from having what we say we want, and we'll get into some of those throughout this book. But one of my favorite ways of accessing the light and a more expansive version of who we are is redirecting our attention to our soulful needs. One way I learned to do this with myself was by getting really quiet and going within, into those feelings of distress and disappointment that were associated with my painful relationships. I asked myself how I felt and if I could discover a deeper, more authentic need that I was somehow not meeting. I recognized that I felt unheard, unloved, and unworthy. I realized, more than anything, that I wanted to help other people who felt the same way; that is, I wanted them to feel heard, loved, and worthy in my presence. Now, so many years later, this is the essence of the service I offer the world. And this is the kind of service that always leads me to the highest version of myself. When I give my presence and unconditional love to others, my soul doesn't give a shit about being rejected! That's because I'm in my divine light, not entangled in the human story—which is often bogged down in giving for the sake of receiving something in return, or of finally feeling worthy.

The light within is not concerned with rejection but with what you have to offer from your deepest, truest, most abundant essence. The universe always takes care of you in this process.

Now, every time I feel misaligned with my true north, disconnected, troubled, or just "not right," I think about my most powerful soulful need and my driving force: being of service. I focus on what I can do to help others—and to be honest, it probably does as much for me as it does for the people I come in contact with. I know that I'm living my purpose because my way of being has ripple effects that create more light in the world. I know if everyone on this planet feels whole and is living in their own version of divinity, the global issues so many of us are trying to solve simply wouldn't exist.

I want to emphasize that, like anything else, recognizing and meeting your soulful needs takes some practice. It took a lot of trial and error to recognize how I could start meeting my soulful needs in a more direct and meaningful way that didn't cause harm to me or others, so just by reading this book, you're lessening the time it'll take for you to do the same thing, since I went first and figured out where the potholes were! I also came to see that all of us have a built-in "alarm" system—when something in our lives isn't working, the alarm goes off, not to scare us but to give us feedback that redirects our attention to a more constructive way of being in the world. It is what we do with that alarm that determines the outcome.

There will be times when soulful needs show up and we try to address them incorrectly—for example, when the need for creativity gets trapped in an exciting, well-paying job that sounds amazing on the surface but that actually stifles the deeper desire to express ourselves more authentically. This doesn't mean we've done something wrong. Lack of fulfillment is just feedback that we're seeing things through a limited human story and that it's time to expand, to bring it back to basics, and to come home to our light.

## PRACTICE: GET IN TOUCH
## WITH YOUR SOULFUL NEEDS

1.  Identify your soulful needs. Do this by responding to the following questions:

    *When do you feel most like yourself? When are you happiest and at peace in your life? What is it that you're embodying when this happens?*

    Remember, a soulful need isn't an external action; it's an internal quality that you feel and embody. Asking yourself these questions is a great starting point for identifying what your soulful needs are—and sometimes, it takes identifying what you *don't* want or what *doesn't* fulfill you to get to what you do want and what *does* fulfill you.

2.  If you're having trouble identifying your soulful needs, chisel them down. Do you remember an experience of feeling whole, perhaps when you were a child, before any traumas took over and hijacked your consciousness? Is there a specific need that feels as if it consistently goes unmet in certain areas of your life? If so, what do you think the soulful need behind that neglected need is? Even if you can only bring to mind a single moment or a vague example, identify it. It helps to be as concrete as possible as you gently immerse yourself in your memory, bringing in all your senses so that you can really feel it and connect to the soulful need that's hidden there.

3. Refer to the list of soulful needs you identified in question 1.

4. If it's possible, hone the list down to a single soulful need. Maybe it's service, or open-hearted communication, or freedom. You don't need to know how to fulfill this need just yet. Simply focus on the feeling associated with the soulful need. Let it fill your heart space.

5. Now, create a list of ways to address your number-one soulful need. You'll continue to refine what "fulfillment" looks like for you, but the point of this activity is to come up with tangible ways to meet that soulful need in your daily life on an ongoing basis. When you practically and consistently fulfill this soulful need, it will become your dominant reality, and the rest of your life will be built around it. Remember, all we need is access to a pinprick of the divine light to create our most expansive, wise, creative, loving reality.

## YOUR DIVINE LIGHT PRACTICE

Do the *Get in Touch with Your Soulful Needs* practice again. This time you may wish to light a candle and create a sacred, peaceful space for this process. Take some time to really walk through and understand your top soulful needs, boiling it all down to the one at the center of your life, which is such a huge part of your personal manifestation of the light within. Think of this soulful need as the key that turns the ignition in your life. When you come up with your list of ways to meet that soulful need, post it somewhere visible, so that you're always reminded that you have so many ways of expanding into your divine light!

Also, take time to revisit the reflection questions at the end of each section in this chapter and journal on them. They're designed to help you uncover the ways you might be getting bogged down in your human story, and to give you the awareness you need to shift more readily into the light within.

The process of
living in our light
is, quite simply, a
process of conscious
recollection, where
we are always
working to come
back to ourselves.

## Takeaways

1. The first pathway of light is **expansion**. To come back into a state of wholeness, happiness, and connection with yourself and the world around you, all it takes is your willingness to expand your perspective by asking a simple question: *Am I living in the darkness, or am I reaching toward the light?*

2. There are several ways to discern whether you're stuck in your human story and haven't yet expanded into your divine light:

   a. You tend to focus on external circumstances over your internal state of being and the lessons you've learned.

   b. You feel like a victim to your circumstances.

   c. You continue to self-sabotage in your life and to fall back on toxic habits and patterns of behavior—usually, because there's some part of you that doesn't believe it deserves to be happy.

   d. You feel broken inside, like there's some part of you that needs fixing before you could ever be truly fulfilled and live your best life.

   e. You tend to think and intellectualize your way into and out of a situation, rather than inviting greater vulnerability and a heart-centered approach to life.

3. The ability to expand into your divine light is connected to your capacity for surrender. Simply being willing to walk into your fear of the unknown expands your trust in yourself and the universe.

4. When it feels like the divine is too far away or inaccessible, slow down, breathe, and come back to simplicity. You don't need to figure everything out all at once! Just give yourself space to surrender, and let the magic reveal itself to you.

5. One of the best ways to open up to and expand into the light within is to acknowledge and honor your soulful needs—deep inner compasses that orient you to who you really are and what your soul desires to express and emanate in this lifetime.

# CHAPTER 2

# self-knowledge

One of the biggest problems I see in the world is the tendency to make every problem mean something about ourselves, which leads to generating a false identity that keeps us from bravely embracing who we really are. The second pathway of light, **self-knowledge**, helps you to discover the freedom that comes from a very simple realization: it's not all about you! Part of the human experience of suffering is that we find it difficult to accept when something bad is happening; instead, we internalize it to mean that something is wrong with us. We create negative interpretations that place ourselves at the center rather than simply responding to any situation, "bad" or "good," with our wholehearted presence and awareness. We end up building an entire identity around our perceived sense of inadequacy. It's only when we stop making our challenges mean something negative about us that we produce the emotional frequency of empowerment—which can only happen with the self-knowledge that we are infinite, divine beings having a finite, human experience. With that, we are able to recognize that, as infinite beings, we can actually *do* something about the situation—and even if the outcome isn't "perfect," we can honor ourselves for having done our best. As humans, there are human matters we must deal with, and self-knowledge can keep us from sinking in the garbage of limiting stories. It can also help us face the world with an open heart that is not stuck in false beliefs about who we are and of what we're capable.

The opposite of self-knowledge tends to look like an inflated or deflated ego. When we overidentify with certain situations in our lives, either "good" or "bad" according to our perception, we are mistaking the things that have *happened* to us for who we fundamentally *are*. We tend to define ourselves using the human story, which can lead us to unconsciously relate every negative experience to some kind of personal shortcoming or flaw in our basic way of being. When we do this, it triggers a signal to our unconscious mind that says something like, "Oh, here I go again, being my usual irresponsible, spacey, oversensitive, weird, angry (fill in the blank with your chosen form of self-judgment) self again!" This doesn't do us any favors, as it usually ends up magnetizing more experiences that cause us to draw similar conclusions about ourselves. What's worse—we turn them into an identity! Our self-judgment can also lead to anxiety and even depression. What will benefit us most is to turn our self judgment to self-awareness, which is what leads to self-knowledge. With so much energy focused on ourselves, it's easier to use that observation for productive outcomes instead of continuing the cycle of self-sabotage.

I once received an unexpected IRS bill in the mail. At the time, I had this identity that was fixated on following all the rules, including paying my bills on time—because the reason my family ended up without a home around the time I was born was that my parents had improperly managed our taxes. You can probably imagine that my "always follow the rules" identity was pretty flustered and upset!

I've since talked to dozens of people who were also slapped with an unwanted IRS bill . . . and who reacted in much the same way I did. That is, they automatically went into negative thinking, berating themselves with a self-defeating inner monologue. "I'm so irresponsible! I didn't file my taxes correctly, and now this is going to ruin my life. How could I have been so stupid?" (I've heard other reactions that turn an external situation into just an aspect of identity, like letting IRS notices pile up and doing nothing about it. Such avoidance conveys the unconscious message, "Facing this head-on is too hard. I'm the kind of person who can't handle an IRS bill.")

Words have power: they can be blessings or they can be weapons—and the conversation we have with ourselves 24/7 often reveals how our language builds us up or breaks us down. I often suggest to my clients and students that they replace "I am" with "I behaved in a way that feels" whenever they find themselves being sucked down a spiral of harsh, critical, or downright abusive thoughts. This creates greater freedom in how we respond to difficult circumstances. So, instead of getting paralyzed around a perceived sense of irresponsibility and stupidity, as well as a gloomy (and probably unrealistic) picture of what will happen, I could reframe my IRS experience and say, "Wow, I guess I made a lot more money than expected— how cool! Maybe I should have been watching my profit and loss more closely, but at least I know I have the power to fix the situation. And I assume responsibility for that."

Can you feel the difference between this way of thinking and the previous example of spinning out in negativity? There's so much more room for resolution when we give ourselves the grace and space to find it . . . or let it find us! Miraculously, I learned that my accountant had grossly miscalculated my additional expenses—but in my favor! It was only when I shifted into a more empowering story and surrendered to what was showing up that I decided to do a little digging. The initial bill had me so panicked that I fell into a small, fearful part of myself that was definitely not a problem solver, and it certainly didn't have multiple perspectives on the issue. I had to shift into a bigger story before I could even dig up the missing information. This also opened me up to a new accounting team that was more capable of handling the level of income I was earning—and because of their knowledge, my taxes moving forward looked wonderful!

It's only when we stop making our challenges mean something negative about us that we produce the emotional frequency of empowerment. We recognize that, as infinite beings, we can actually do something about the situation—and even if the outcome isn't "perfect," we can trust that we did our best. (We'll talk about how we can practice this toward the end of the chapter.) Bad stuff happens all the time, and sure, some of that might be related to choices we made in the past. But no choice is set in stone, and we can always make different ones. Our choices might shape our reality, but even the disempowering ones are not ultimately who we are deep down. We belong to a divine awareness that, if we tune in to it, reminds us we are always whole and perfect as we are (and I'm not talking "perfect" in terms of all the external stuff that might signal we have our lives together—I'm talking about the *soul,* which is way bigger than the ego!). Simply stepping into this awareness can help us to navigate the pitfalls of life that all of us are sure to run into at some point or other.

Believe me, lots of terrible things have happened to me. But I don't walk around telling people, "I'm a rape victim," or, "I'm someone who didn't pay my tax bill in the right way," as if these experiences could possibly define and contain *the rainbow of me* (to borrow my husband Oliver's term). Sure, these experiences are a part of my human story, but it's what I do with them that ultimately defines me in this lifetime. And, oddly enough, the perspective shift often changes the outcome or reality altogether (more on that in the final practice section of this chapter).

Dear soul, I'm here to tell you: You are much bigger than everything that's happened to you. I understand that some of it, traumatic or joyful, has shaped you in major ways, but there's no way it defines you—even if you've been using said experiences to create a negative interpretation of your life and your potential. But I get it! We are biologically wired to remember and internalize our experiences and to conveniently forget the shiny, divine mirror that periodically gives us a glimpse into the depth of our beautiful souls. It's a human tendency to bounce reality back on ourselves to make sense of it, because we just love constructs so much! A beautiful aspect of the human story is the need to understand ourselves and the world around us. But the bouncing-off doesn't have to be about getting bruised and mangled in a school of hard knocks. As always, we can choose to ask, "What else could this mean?"

## THE MYTH OF FAILURE AND PERFECTIONISM

One of the biggest myths that keeps us mired in our human story is that we just aren't good enough because we've failed at this thing called life in countless different ways. If only we'd been and acted perfectly, perhaps we would have escaped the pain and shame and disappointment of the horrible experiences that served to twist the knife of self-hatred deeper into our hearts. We come to identify with this story of failure, even when it has absolutely nothing to do with us (and even though so-called failure is the number one thing most people universally regarded as successful have stated was their greatest teacher).

I went through a string of dysfunctional relationships before meeting my wonderful husband, Oliver. One particular relationship was especially painful; my partner was manipulative, and he constantly lied and cheated on me. There were times when I intuited that he'd cheated, and when I'd bring up my suspicions, he'd simply deflect by shooting back with something mean and undercutting. Instead of taking this to mean that my suspicions had been confirmed, I turned it into a story of "I'm not good enough—which is why he's so mean and continues to cheat" and so on. I didn't think to say, "Wow . . . here's this lost, insecure person in front of me, and I can see all that ugliness playing out. It has nothing to do with me, and it probably existed well before I came along!"

I later learned that this man had been through a lot of trauma, which had likely caused him to act out in ugly ways and to project his own self-loathing onto his romantic partners and others. But did I take any of that into account when I made the decision to create an identity of "not-good-enough failure" on the basis of his poor treatment? Nope! Again, the part of me that wanted so badly to understand what was happening naturally made myself a part of his story. My understanding didn't have to conclude with "there's something wrong with me," but let me tell you—when you're in a relationship with a toxic person, it can be really difficult not to make their treatment mean something bad about you, especially if the relationship started with lots of love and affection. I'd also later come to discover what *love bombing*, was—excessive attention and affection (especially at the beginning of a connection). This is a very real thing that energy vampires and unconscious people do to gain control over the people in their lives. It's often followed by dangling the same carrot of adoration in front of another person, only to yank it away and make them dependent on you. Sound messed up? Totally. And is it about the person who's victimized by the behavior? Not at all! But like I said, it's really hard to see the forest for the trees when you're stuck in the emotional reactivity of the human story, which tends to operate on tunnel vision!

I'd like to take a moment here to point out that I'm not a fan of how certain words like *energy vampire* and *narcissist* get thrown around willy-nilly nowadays, as we are, in essence, villainizing someone who is unhealed. But, for the sake of understanding, sometimes those words help us explain certain characteristics that have become coping mechanisms for some people. I hope you choose to see that there's beauty in all people, even those who behave in toxic and hurtful ways, and who have chosen to express the unhealed version of themselves. Have I been toxic in relationships? Maybe not to the extent I've experienced from others, but I've certainly behaved badly to protect myself from certain situations. This was always the result of pain inflicted on me. Let's never forget that empathy, which we'll learn about in Chapter 3, is vital in helping us maintain an expanded view of even the most seemingly toxic and difficult people.

If you've been where I've been—in a state of "not enough" that has kept you trapped in unfulfilling relationships—I ask that you be oh, so gentle with yourself. I know it can be easy to turn "I'm not good enough" into the future story "Damn, I should've known better." They're variations on the same myth that we should have had it all figured out in advance! But once again, I remind you that living in the light isn't about being "perfect," or not having emotions, or knowing all the answers when you're stuck in a bad situation. It's about giving yourself kindness and digging yourself out of the hole with tiny but effective questions, like my favorite: "What else could this mean?"

A good friend who's a child psychiatrist once told me, "Mandy, the one thing I consistently see in young children is that they tend to perceive they're not enough." It's an incorrect interpretation that we tend to take with us all the way into adulthood. The thing is, while it's totally wrong, it's understandable that we have it. For lots of us, this perception, which comes from reflecting other people's reactions and behaviors back on ourselves, is a survival technique. Those of us who grew up in abusive or unpredictable environments used it to gain a sense of control, since some part of us probably intuited (albeit in a twisted way) that the only thing we can control is us. So, if we changed ourselves to fit what we thought someone else wanted, maybe that would keep us safe. This incorrect perception continues to keep us stuck as adults until we start chipping away at it to discover that it's hollow underneath.

This is where I want to say that there are absolutely times when it's appropriate to internalize a screwup we've made and to do something about it. For example, if you lose your job because you fail to go into work for seven days in a row without informing your boss about that action, there's probably some cleaning up you have to do! And if you're engaging in patterns that negatively impact you and others, you can take a good, hard look at why this is happening and start to do something about it!

However, I've found that overidentifying with the behavior actually gives us an excuse to *not* do anything about it! Remember my IRS fiasco and the person who ignores the pileup of tax notices, defaulting to the identity of being too incompetent to do anything about it? So often, we can flip-flop between "I should have known (or/done) better and not failed," and "Oh well, guess I just suck, and that's the end of that!" This doesn't leave much of an opening for transformation, does it?

I always talk about the importance of turning our so-called failures into opportunities. Sarah Blakely, the founder of the women's clothing company Spanx, has a story about how at night, her dad would ask everyone in the family about what they'd failed at that day. In fact, he encouraged them to do what they perceived themselves to be "bad" at, so they were always challenging themselves to get outside their comfort zone. I love this story so much, because I think it shows a great way to correct our faulty perception of failure and what it does or doesn't mean about us. It helps us to navigate challenges with greater facility and to see the opportunities within them for turning back to the light that is our soul essence.

You may be familiar with the Thomas Edison quote, "I have not failed. I've just found 10,000 ways that wouldn't work." There's so much power in learning what doesn't work! When we cling to perfectionism, it's like seeing a star in the sky that's billions of light-years away and incorrectly assuming that this tiny pinprick is all the light there is! We forget the infinite spectrum of experience that exists beyond the human story—all the interpretations of what's happening in our lives that could serve to empower us rather than pull us down.

I want to be clear here that *empowering* is the key word! It's not useful to rewrite a painful story, like the one of my dysfunctional relationship, in a way that keeps us further stuck. For example, someone could distort the idea of embracing failure to say, "My partner is obviously hurting, so instead of taking it personally, I can just be more loving to him." That's like swapping one disempowering identity ("not good enough") for another ("savior"). Remember, you can't save someone who doesn't want to save themselves, especially if that means continuing to put yourself in the line of abuse.

If you find yourself continually trying to "get it right" in a situation or relationship, take a step back to really examine how that's working out for you. You'll probably see that this attitude isn't yielding the result you want. You're employing a false perception of control that enables you to avoid your pain. All humans run from pain and toward pleasure—we're wired as such—but when we focus too much on running away, we lose out on the essence of life, like a great relationship or job opportunity. Someone once said, "Hell on earth is meeting the person you could've been." Confronting our pain helps us to recognize the opportunities hiding in plain sight. More than that, it helps us to step into the light . . . by helping us to see that it's possible to fail and to *still* be enough.

In many ways, I think a lot of us end up failing at perfectionism because our soul doesn't actually want us to be perfect. Heck, no! How boring would that be? Our soul has given us a fail-safe; whatever we attempt to accomplish through control and perfectionism will eventually fall apart because the soul is in search of its wholeness. It doesn't want to accomplish anything via control or to live by arbitrary rules. That's why failure isn't a sign that there's something wrong with us! It's a sign that there's a better way to go about meeting our needs, and it's up to us to find it.

## Reflection Questions

1. In what ways do you feel you aren't "good enough"? Is there a relationship pattern or experience that serves to keep this feeling in motion?

2. How do you use the identity of "not good enough" as an excuse not to transform or level up in your life, or to have more fulfilling relationships?

3. Can you remember a time when you failed but then experienced a major breakthrough that helped you access more of your divine light? How can you reframe a recent experience of "failure" in this way?

## THE BALL AND CHAIN
## THAT CAN SET US FREE

Having a chosen identity, or multiple chosen identities, is absolutely not a bad thing! Often, it can be really beautiful and empowering, especially if it connects us to a beloved community that helps us access even more of our gifts. You might identify as a woman, an artist, an immigrant, a healer, a businessperson, or any number of things that, for you, represents so much more than just labels, they're soul callings. These are the kinds of identities that connect us more deeply to our light, and when it comes down to it, they're also big enough to hold the rainbow of who we are.

But on the flip side, an identity can also be a ball and chain that unwittingly rules our life and limits our potential. It can be perpetually connected to the feeling that we just aren't good enough (even if that identity is perceived as "good," like being a successful businessperson or beautiful or smart or talented—which are awesome, but can also lock us into a never-ending battle of questioning our true worth). We always have to ask ourselves why we've taken on these identities. For example, if my "why" for wanting to help others is to make them proud of me . . . well, that's a pretty crappy reason, because it's rooted in the idea that if I just do XYZ, I'll be good enough.

Your divine light helps you see that you're never not good enough. Even when you're struggling, it's not because you're a terrible person, but because you probably haven't claimed every last inch of your authenticity.

Again, the identity you're dragging around like dead weight is nothing if not an opportunity to step into authenticity, to love yourself first and foremost and learn the soulful lesson that the heaviness is trying to teach you.

One of my clients, Wayne, was a successful entrepreneur who had a chain of health shops all over the country. He came to do one-on-one work with me years ago, because he had an issue with his weight and self-image—which was actually why he loved all things healthy. At the same time, he couldn't seem to get past his perception of himself as being far below the physical ideal he wished to live up to. This manifested in him going to the beach and refusing to take his shirt off because he was too ashamed.

"I'd love for you to get to the point where you can take off your shirt without feeling you want to crawl out of your skin," I told him.

"I know," he sighed. "I feel like a broken record, but I don't know what to do. I've struggled with my weight my entire life, and I just want to be over it!"

We worked together for a short while, until he was able to see that while the weight might be really good at getting his attention and making him self-identify as both an "out-of-shape guy" and "that guy who's always trying to be healthy," it wasn't the real issue. The weight was just a way of drawing his awareness to the importance of true, deep self-love. Wayne shared that his mother had always been critical of him, which, of course, translated to ugly comments about his body—which Wayne wrongly came to identify as a commentary on his actual worth.

Once Wayne was able to see this, he had a huge epiphany. He called me excitedly and said, "Holy crap, Mandy! I just realized that weight isn't merely this thing I've struggled with my whole life. It's actually my guru! Weight is the thing that teaches me everything I need to learn. I just wasn't getting what the actual lesson was."

As soon as Wayne stopped seeing his weight as the issue, he didn't have to keep struggling or self-identifying with it. As he came to sit with the love he had for himself, the actual energetic weight of his poor self-esteem came off. Only when he came to the realization that the thing he truly wanted wasn't to be thinner or fitter, but to know his worth beyond a shadow of a doubt, did weight stop being an issue for him.

Wayne's weight issue had become his own personal ball and chain that he dragged along with him wherever he went. Sure, it was part of the reason he had started his health-food chain, but more often than not, it made him feel miserable because he'd become a prisoner to it. It was only when he was able to really see his weight as a teacher pointing him to something much deeper—the power of unconditional self-love—that he was able to step out of that identity, once and for all.

In many ways, Wayne's success story reflected that his chosen method to try to control his life wasn't working. He wanted to be thinner and fitter, but he could never really get there. I suspect that if he'd successfully attained his desired outcome, he might be even more imprisoned in the identity of "fit guy," and there would never have been a need to search for the deeper issue and find the gift in the struggle.

I honestly think it's almost better when a person's chosen control system doesn't work—because that usually means they're not able to meet their needs in higher-vibration ways. They're much too seduced by the rewards that their human story has garnered for them. They've built an airtight persona that feels unsafe to venture out of. And because we live in a freewill universe, when I meet these kinds of people, I wish them well and send them off with love. I know that sooner or later, the persona will crumble (whether in this lifetime or the next), and they'll have the chance to step into their authentic light.

## Reflection Questions

1. What are the airtight personas or identities you've built around your own life? How have they served and/or hindered you?

2. Think of something you've struggled with that you've turned into an identity (e.g., maybe you always describe yourself as "broke" or "bad at relationships")? What might this struggle be shining a light on?

3. How could this struggle actually be your guru, leading the way to a sense of purpose and whatever is important for your soul to learn in this lifetime?

## HONORING YOUR HUMAN NEEDS WITHOUT GETTING STUCK IN THEM

Despite the title of this chapter, self-knowledge is not about the kind of disassociation or escapism in spiritual communities that commonly conflate "knowing who you are" with stripping yourself of your human identity. Self-knowledge is also not about shoving the responsibility of our day-to-day lives onto a "higher power" instead of taking meaningful action toward our goals. As humans, there are human matters we must deal with (hello, IRS bill!). But we can face the world and our lives without leaning on our limiting stories about who we are and what we're capable of. Self-knowledge is actually what helps us shine our light brightly, with an open heart—because it helps us to find empowering ways to meet our human needs.

Our human needs must be met for us to have space for more spiritual or self-actualizing experiences. Escapism is what happens when we deny our human needs—which are things like safety, positive relationships, a sense of trust in ourselves, and a feeling of meaning and purpose in the work we do for a living.

In contrast to a human need, a soulful need is always pure and exists for the purpose of serving humanity and helping us to evolve into the highest versions of ourselves. A human need is also distinct from a soulful need because it falls within the 3D, physical world in some way. Although human needs can help further our spiritual development, they are often expressed in a way that docsn't serve us. Depending on our unique life story and temperament, our human needs will vary, but they fundamentally point to the kind of safety and stability that are necessary for us to flourish in our lives. All of that stuff is what makes life beautiful! It's just that the way we go about meeting those needs can really mess us up.

Let's briefly look at the human need to be heard. Someone might meet this need by screaming at and berating their partner—but over time, perhaps they are able to transmute this behavior and end up journaling to contact their higher power, instead of fueling the angry inner tyrant within them.

One of my deepest human needs is connection. Part of my human story was that, growing up, it felt unsafe to experience true connection. As I got older, the safest way to connect with someone I was in a relationship with was intimacy—often, with toxic partners. Predictably, this was a terrible way to meet the need for connection. Intimacy became a bargaining chip to manipulate my way into temporarily getting what I thought I wanted—which wasn't even real connection to begin with, because it came with strings attached. Even when I was in a committed relationship, I was afraid to open my heart, be vulnerable, or communicate honestly, because that meant I was risking rejection and opening a can of emotional worms I couldn't close. I eventually saw that my desire for connection was so good and so pure and so fundamental to my light . . . and the way I went about getting it made all the difference.

Remember my story about Wayne? It's a great example of how we might think our initial need (in his case, the need to lose weight) is the real one, but if we dig a little deeper, we'll uncover an even truer need (like his desire for authentic self-acceptance and unconditional self-love).

I've similarly had other clients who come to me swearing up and down that there's a specific need they're trying to meet, but it's just not happening! I'm never here to try to get my clients to want a different outcome for themselves, but their intention behind it might need to shift, especially if their desire is to live from their divine story. An intention like "I just want to look good on the outside" is fine, but it's low vibrational compared to "I just want to love myself, no matter what."

This brings up an important lesson about intentional energy, which I often talk about whenever I'm teaching the fundamentals of manifestation. I always say, "The outcome doesn't have to change, but the intention behind it might." For example, perhaps we realize that our intention for wanting the new car or house is so that we'll finally feel like we're good enough. We can gradually shift this intention to wanting something beautiful because it adds to the abundance we've already created. It is our intentional energy—aka our "why"—that matters the most. When the why comes from a higher space of expansion instead of being a means to an end or so we can fit into a box, it is of a high vibration. It helps us get to the heart of the deeper need, which is the experience of unconditional love. When we change our intention, the outcome may or may not shift—but when we're rooted in what our soul wants for us, we'll get the result that meets the deeper need that's trying to get our attention.

The outcome doesn't
have to change,
but the intention
behind it might.

I always envisioned a house on a hill as my dream home. It would have both ocean and mountain views with big windows. My "why," which was buried deep inside me, was that once I had my dream home, I would finally be good enough and the people who told me I wouldn't amount to anything would be wowed. Years later, as I worked out on my elliptical outside my home in Laguna Beach, pregnant with one of my children, I realized I was living in my dream house. The waves were crashing on the hill in front of me, and a mountain range was to my left. My intention had changed without me even realizing it! The house came to fruition because it was a beautiful home that matched my energy of love and service, and because I was living in my light as much as I could. However, I hadn't willed the house into existence. It had simply "appeared"!

When this happens, as Wayne discovered, the human part of us is finally satisfied and at peace. That tends to happen when we meet our human needs in elevated, pro-active, healthy ways (and when we're encouraged to actually value and honor our human needs, which many of us are not taught to do). We feel more confident and sure of ourselves, and more capable of shining our light more brightly in the world. This hearkens back to psychologist Abraham Maslow's famous hierarchy of needs—a theory of human motivation where Maslow suggested that meeting our basic human needs makes it easier for us to meet our more spiritual needs. But again, the way we go about meeting our human needs matters, because it can be the key that determines whether or not we'll unlock our access to the light within.

## Reflection Questions

1.  What are some of your personal human needs that give you a sense of safety and connection to yourself and others?

2.  Can you think of a time when you tried to meet one of those needs in a way that ended up being painful? Why do you think that was?

3.  Think about a human need you are trying to meet now that doesn't seem to be achievable. Gently ask yourself if there might be a higher-vibration way to meet this need that you haven't tried yet.

## STIMULUS, THOUGHT, REACTION, OUTCOME

Remember my monk friend who said, "The purpose of life is life, mon!"? Essentially, he was asking me to lighten up!

I know this is a tall order for many of us, especially when we look around and see all the pain and suffering in the world. Again, this is a great opportunity to think of how we can alleviate that pain and suffering—but we don't have to become a part of it by getting our energy entangled in its heavy field.

When I was younger, I made mountains out of mole-hills. Every little challenge felt like it was at a 10. This is how we lose ourselves. We get so caught up in and identified with the turmoil, we forget this is literally just a blip in time—a pinprick of reality.

You might be wondering: *Well, how in the world does someone just get lighter? Isn't that easier said than done?*

And my answer is: *Nope!* It's all about taking five steps back and getting into the neutral zone. We all live on an emotional spectrum that takes us all the way from hopelessness to joy—smack dab in the middle is neutrality, which feels a lot like curiosity. If I find myself sitting in the human world, identifying with it, or making it mean something about me, this is a sign that I need to get curious. Even if it feels like everything is falling apart, I remind myself that it's just feedback. It's not what's happening that defines my life or gets to orchestrate my outcome—it's all about what I choose to do with it. (I always tell the practitioners and therapists I certify that we don't get emotional—we get curious!)

I call this method Stimulus, Thought, Reaction, Outcome, or STRO for short. It's a remarkable practice that I've used with millions of clients and students.

During one of my retreats, a participant, Maggie, was really upset with the group. Her inner wounded child had been triggered at breakfast when Dave, a man with really expressive, wide eyes, talked over her when she was right in the middle of saying something. She was sure, judging by the expression on his face, that he had totally dissed her and didn't care what she had to say. This was so troubling to Maggie that, instead of enjoying breakfast with this loving group of people, she locked herself in her room and pouted about the experience for most of the day.

Later that afternoon, during a workshop, she decided she wanted to talk about and process what had happened. She directed her attention at Dave and said, "I was really hurt by what you did this morning when you ignored what I was saying and talked over me. It ruined my day, and now I can't help but replay it and think of all the times this has happened to me in the past."

Dave was genuinely shocked—he didn't remember the story the way Maggie was telling it! He listened to her as she shared her pain, and then he said, "Just so you know, Maggie, this is the way I look all the time. I thought you were done talking, and there was so much commotion in the dining room, I guess I didn't realize you weren't done—which is why I started talking to someone else. I'm so sorry about that, because it was definitely not my intention to cause you pain."

We slowed it down to figure out what had happened, since this was a learning moment for all of us. Here's how I broke it down:

- **Stimulus:** The stimulus, or trigger, was a combination of the way Dave had looked at Maggie and how he'd subsequently turned away to talk to someone else while she was still communicating with him.

- **Thought:** Maggie's immediate thought was: Dave doesn't care about me, and the look in his eyes and his behavior totally prove it!

- **Reaction:** Maggie's reaction was to totally shut down because that single thought propelled her into painful memories of similar past experiences in which she'd felt unseen, unheard, and not valued.

- **Outcome:** Maggie lost half a day of information and the opportunity to bond with the group. Instead, she'd sat in her room and sulked, which made her feel even worse.

STRO is a great tool for developing our awareness, because most of us don't realize it's not the stimulus that leads to the outcome. That is, Dave wasn't responsible for Maggie's experience. Rather, it was her *thought* and her *reaction* that led to the experience of alienation she'd felt from the group. And being alienated, as it turned out, was an identity that Maggie had carried around with her for years.

Like Maggie, many of us don't stop to recognize that our thoughts and reactions are responsible for the experiences we end up having and the way we feel about ourselves and our lives. This is a good example of how we get so wrapped up and identified with our thoughts that we don't see the outcomes they're producing.

When we walked through this process, step by step, Maggie began to realize that everything she'd experienced was part of what she was bringing to the table. There was a closed-off part of her that was running the show and that ended up getting her into situations that only confirmed that people were against her. "I tend to look through this lens of 'nobody likes me' whenever I'm in a new environment," she observed. Thankfully, Dave taking it on himself to say that, in fact, he *did* like her helped her to see that her thoughts and reactions weren't aligned with the reality of what had happened. Maggie went through a palpable shift after that. Her energy was so big, bright, and contagious that it filled up the room in the best way possible for the remainder of the retreat.

At the end of it all, she said, "This was such a positive experience for me, because it really helped me to ask myself: *How often am I looking at life incorrectly? How am I not seeing myself accurately?*" She learned that she could authentically choose a different thought and a different reaction to the same kind of stimulus—and then she'd change the outcome altogether.

## PRACTICE: STIMULUS, THOUGHT, REACTION, OUTCOME

This tool will help you interrogate your usual outcomes and to consider how you might be able to reach a totally different outcome. As you walk through this process, please note that it isn't about blaming or shaming yourself for any past painful experiences. It's about empowering yourself to get the outcomes that will help you meet your human needs in the most divine way possible! Again, a need isn't bad and it must be met—but how we go about meeting it is the most important thing.

1.  Think of a stimulus that triggers you. For the sake of simplicity, don't choose anything that's too triggering or that is casting a huge shadow over your life in the present moment. Choose something that has triggered you for a long time and that you know will probably come up at some point in the near future. For example, your mom's tone of voice when she inquires about your love life (you know, *that* tone that never fails to set off an alarm somewhere inside you), or your partner's tendency to never replace the toilet paper when they use up the roll, or your boss's habit of bombarding you with e-mail after e-mail when you're busy.

2.  What thought usually comes to mind after the stimulus arises? Sometimes, we assume our thoughts are the objective truth without realizing that it's our thinking that usually gets us into hot water! Maybe in the examples offered above, the split-second thought is "Mom is always so damn judgmental," or "Ugh, there my partner goes,

being irresponsible and not considering how their behavior impacts me," or, "My boss really doesn't respect me or believe in my competence."

3.  How do you react after you have that thought? The thought is very much linked to the reaction we express, either inwardly or outwardly, and the person we end up believing we are. Maybe you don't say anything to your mom when she asks you a question in a critical tone, but you beat yourself up over it all weekend by wallowing as you binge-watch bad TV shows. Maybe you yell at your partner for being so inconsiderate. Maybe you feel paranoid that your boss is going to fire you, so you bend over backward and exhaust yourself by working even harder.

4.  When you display these behaviors, what's the outcome? Maybe Mom notices you're falling into a pit of despair and criticizes you more overtly next time. Or maybe your partner gets defensive and reminds you that you're not exactly perfect, and it starts a huge fight. Perhaps your boss notices that their constant needling keeps you alert and responsive, so they keep doing it without even realizing how you feel.

    a.  Be honest with yourself. Does your outcome take you where you want to go, externally speaking?

    b.  Internally speaking, what is the story that this entire STRO process has you telling about yourself? Using the examples above it might be, "I'm bad at dating and I'm gonna die alone"; "I'm such a nag and my partner never listens to me anyway, so what's the point?"; and "My boss continues to undermine and undervalue me, even though I put in so much, so it just goes to show I'm a push-over." It's okay to exaggerate for the purpose of this exercise. But try to get at the core of how you might be identifying with stories in ways that impact you negatively.

5. Now that you can see how your thought and reaction are linked to your internal and external outcomes, it's time to take back your power.

   a. Start by asking yourself: *What's the need I'm trying to fulfill?* (Based on the examples above, maybe the need is loving communication, respect, or trust.)

   b. Then ask: *Is the way I'm going about it (based on the outcomes I tend to get) empowering or disempowering, healthy or unhealthy, part of my human story or my divine story?* (Also based on the examples above, you're likely to see that your reaction is hurting you and possibly those around you.)

   c. Give yourself genuine love and appreciation for asking these questions. The pursuit of self-knowledge can be scary, but it's deeply fulfilling and exciting when you have the frequency of light supporting you! Feel the divine light opening up and loving the heck out of you!

d. Take the proverbial five steps back and detach from the emotion that tends to accompany the stimulus, which is responsible for the thoughts you create. Based on the need you identified, what could a healthier, more loving thought look like? For example, maybe your thought is, "Mom wants me to be happy, even though she has a tough time expressing that," or, "There they go again, not replacing the toilet roll. It's really funny that they keep forgetting!" or, "It might be more efficient to talk about these issues with my boss during a meeting instead of responding to all these e-mails. Why don't I suggest that, so I can keep working on my task?"

e. You've done the hard part. Now that you've identified the new thought, what might a new reaction be? It'll be easier to select a new reaction by reconnecting with the deep need you're trying to meet. With the examples I've mentioned, it could be as simple as sharing your thoughts with the person, because you want more open communication. Or maybe you decide that none of these matters are so serious that you need to do anything about them (which is totally your prerogative). The more reactions you can come up with, the more choice available to you—which is exactly what the light within wants for you.

You can begin to work with STRO whenever a real-time stimulus comes knocking at your door, and soon you'll be able to detangle negative thoughts and reactions with ease. You'll see that growth doesn't have to be a huge, complicated process, and you don't even have to feel 100 percent better to make progress!

It can be fun and oddly easy to employ this practice; even in the middle of a hard situation, I can definitely get a laugh out of it. You'll find it exciting and gratifying to get to know more parts of yourself in this way and to meet your needs more authentically. STRO always helps us to expand into even more of who we are, and there's always a reward waiting for us on the other side.

## YOUR DIVINE LIGHT PRACTICE

Repeat the *Stimulus, Thought, Reaction, Outcome* practice. This time, you'll want to choose a stimulus that tends to pop up over and over and that you associate with undesirable outcomes. It's also a great exercise for helping you get in touch with your human needs and to meet them in ways that keep you fluid and flexible, instead of caught up in false stories that have you take everything so personally.

As always, take time to revisit the reflection questions at the end of each section in this chapter, and to journal on them.

## Takeaways

1.  If you ever feel overwhelmed by any part of this process, just take a moment to breathe and remember that simply reading this book

is helping you to embody these principles in a deeper way than your conscious mind realizes.

2.  You are so much bigger than anything that's ever happened to you, and you can make the choice to let challenging situations and setbacks offer you feedback on where to go next, instead of entangling them with your core identity. This is how you get to the second pathway of light: **self-knowledge**!

3.  "Failure" is an opportunity to assess where we might be misaligned with our soul. Instead of taking your so-called failures as an excuse to beat yourself up over not being enough (which can keep you from exercising your divine responsibility to transform), ask yourself, *What else might this mean?* and look for the key that will help you unlock your access to light.

4.  If there's an identity you feel stuck in that isn't giving you the outcomes you want (for example, you're "Susie Homemaker" but don't feel appreciated at home), recognize that it's time to go one level deeper, where a totally different lesson awaits you (for example, you've stifled your independence because you're afraid your family will reject you if you follow the path you really dream of taking).

5.  The identity you've tried so hard to fit into always signals a deeper need you aren't meeting in a healthy way.

6.  Self-knowledge emerges from disidentifying
    from harmful stories by using Stimulus,
    Thought, Reaction, Outcome (STRO), which
    helps you to slow down and see how you might
    be incorrectly making your relationships and
    experiences mean something negative about
    you—and to choose thoughts and reactions
    that undermine all of that and get you to
    different outcomes.

# CHAPTER 3

# empathy

As we practice expansion and self-knowledge with even greater facility and willingness, we will naturally ask ourselves the kinds of questions that help us to open our hearts: "What else could this mean?" *This* difficult human experience . . . *this* painful moment . . . *this* pattern that distorts the way we look at the world and makes us feel as twisty as a pretzel, tangled up in all these false ideas about who we really are . . . can truly be viewed in a new way—a way that takes us out of the trap of self-imposed victimhood as we consider the larger panorama of events that is unfolding—which takes us straight into the light.

This chapter is all about the third pathway of light, **empathy**—which, as you'll learn, is not the same as either forgiveness or sympathy. For me, the key to "What else could this mean?" is this—the act of extending understanding to ourselves or to someone in our life. Forgiveness is actually secondary to empathy. When we empathize with someone, especially if we were hurt by them, it doesn't take away the reality that something painful and difficult happened. However, it expands our human story so that we can be free from the resentment and powerlessness that can loom like a storm cloud over our lives when we're caught in questions like "Why me?" Empathy shifts our perspective so that we see with greater clarity. We begin to recognize that the person who harmed us was probably affected by circumstances that had nothing to do with us. They were most likely acting from their own misguided perceptions of the world, patterns, and defense mechanisms.

When it comes to empathy, I can't help but think of my mom. Today, we have an amazing relationship because, together, we've healed so much of our past. However, when I was growing up, my mom and I were at odds. In her attempt to survive, put food on the table, and provide more than what my homeless infancy had given me, she lost herself. I grew up in what felt like a loveless home with a lot of pain coming from various sources. I incorrectly looked at her as the reason, and I blamed her accordingly. It was so bad that at the age of 10, I found myself fighting in court to live with my dad (I had no idea he was an addict and unstable—I just wanted change). I didn't win that battle, and for a number of reasons, anger became my default emotion.

Fast-forward years later: I was an adult when my mother announced that she was divorcing my very unhealthy stepfather, who, unbeknownst to us, had deeply hurt her over the years. No wonder our home had felt loveless.

"Good!" I exclaimed. For once, we were on the same page.

She was genuinely taken aback. "Really? You're okay with this?"

I was confused as to why *she* was so confused. "Of course! I'm *happy* about it, actually!" I told her that all I'd ever wanted was to see a happy version of her—the one that would come out occasionally but quickly melt away under the crippling responsibility of being the family provider. I realized she'd been hiding her pain so she could stay strong. This opened the door to the first honest conversation we'd ever had. We talked about the toxicity that had bound our family for a very long time. She revealed that she had so badly wanted me and my siblings to have a father around who would provide us with some semblance of stability, since my father had left when I was a baby. As I talked our past through with my mother, I understood her in a way I never had before. I had always been so angry with her, but now, I felt I was seeing a glimpse of the hurt hiding beneath the tough exterior. I recognized the trauma she'd lived through from childhood through adulthood; I realized that for most of my life, she'd been in survival mode, turning off her feelings to persevere and "do what needs to be done." Her life had not unfolded according to what she thought would be her plan. But now, the facade was beginning to crack. My mom had come to a place of true strength and was ready to make changes in her life. Behind all that armor, I started to see her light again, as well as her potential and the amazingly gracious spirit who was shining through.

This began a powerful process of mutual healing that we both walked through, side by side. But to get there, I had to let go of my interpretation of my mom as the enemy I'd considered her in my adolescence. (What child doesn't want to villainize a parent?) But she wasn't my enemy. She was a soul attempting to find her path the best way she knew, and in her eyes, so much of what she'd done was for her children. This new perspective helped me to let go of so much of the pain and resentment I still held toward her. Some of this included the anger I had toward our early relationship, as well as the misdirected anger I held in my trauma around my father. He hadn't been around to blame, so she'd unfairly received the brunt of it. Recognizing this freed me of so much extra weight I'd unknowingly been carrying around based on my limited story of who she was. Today, Mom and I have an amazing relationship—one that I could never have imagined as a child or young adult. We talk and laugh and continue to grow, and I wish she lived next door!

Now, exercising empathy does not always lead to a repaired relationship. Today, I can also have empathy for my stepfather, who struggled with the aftereffects of his own severe trauma. I disliked him intensely when I was a child. I hated the punishments he put me through—such as making me scrub the floor with a toothbrush and pick hot rocks out of the sandbox. But, in retrospect, I understand that was his method of exercising control in a life that felt extremely out of control.

The more I began opening to my own light, the more I noticed that every single person has a nuanced story at the heart of all their reasons for doing and being. Mom used to always say, "You can't judge someone unless you've walked a mile in their moccasins."

The truth is, nobody behaves in dark or evil ways by happenstance. There's always a reason, even if you don't know what it is. I've never met a bitter person and thought, *Gee, they must have had a wonderful life!* If someone attacks or abuses other people, there's a reason.

And this is the essence of empathy: It allows us an intimate peek behind the curtain. While whatever we see on the surface might not make a whole lot of sense, there is a more complete story that lives below our limited observations. Opening up to the light within gives us that bigger picture in a way that releases us from suffering and helps us to connect with the infinite source of compassion that leads to healing—not necessarily healing of the relationship itself, but healing of whatever fractures have been created in us as the result of that hurt. Not to mention, the vibrational frequency of empathy sits higher than that of joy, which is why it's so important to integrate into our daily awareness, as it can transmute so much of the toxicity in our lives.

## WHY EMPATHY IS NOT
## THE SAME AS FORGIVENESS

Empathy is not the same as forgiveness. Sometimes, we experience empathy on the path to forgiveness, which is the conscious and deliberate choice to release any feelings of pain or resentment toward someone who has harmed us. Forgiveness can be an amazing gift to offer, but I will never tell someone they need to forgive another person. I've encountered people who've been victims of heinous experiences, and I understand that part of their process might include owning their anger and hurt over what happened. (Heck, my human self wants to go give their abuser a piece of my mind, but my divine self knows better!) It's not always healthy to jump straight into forgiveness, especially if that means spiritually bypassing uncomfortable emotional experiences that need to be fully processed. It's just not for me to say when someone is ready for it.

The beautiful thing about empathy is that it doesn't require forgiveness. When we hold empathy for someone, it's not about denying what we went through or even saying that we're ready to forgive that person. It's being able to entertain a much larger perspective that has enough room for our feelings *and* the clarity required for us to move from our story of victimization and woundedness, and see that most acts of harm occur because of unconsciousness and unhealthy patterns that never got interrupted. We don't have to make up stories about the other person to get to this place of clarity. All we have to do is observe them closely, from the vantage point of the question, "What else might this mean?" This can help us to pause and unhook from the old stories we've told ourselves.

At this point in my journey I can truly acknowledge that anyone who throws negativity or abuse at another person has an internal issue that has nothing to do with the person on the receiving end. When someone lashes out at me, I know not to take it personally. I understand they are going through something I may not know enough about, which helps me keep a clear head and view them as an angry toddler throwing a tantrum over not getting their Popsicle before dinner. It's not for me to pick up what they're putting down, although I'm happy to love them through it with my boundaries intact.

Empathy also differs from forgiveness because while forgiveness is focused on letting go, empathy is focused on understanding. Empathy gives us insight into why someone is the way they are. One need not justify a person's behavior to feel bad for them. Instead, we recognize that if we'd gone through the same experiences as them, we might have made similar decisions. Or sometimes, we realize we would *never* have done what they did, and that's also a blessing (similar to the ways in which people bring generational patterns to an end by consciously not enact-ing them or passing them on to the next generation).

The misconception that empathy and forgiveness are the same could keep people from expanding their per-spective. And many people believe that displaying either is an open invitation for toxic people to smash our win-dows and screw up our lives or justify cruelty. Again, this isn't true. While Mom and I mutually worked on build-ing a relationship beyond our wildest dreams, I lost touch with my stepfather after Mom divorced him, and I had no interest in maintaining any kind of relationship with him as the years went on. I wish him well and pray for him often, and while he no longer has a seat at my table, he has a place in my heart. Empathy actually gave me greater clarity about who he was, in such a way that I knew I could wish him well and understand why he'd done the things he'd done—without putting myself in harm's way ever again.

When we exercise empathy, we don't stop having compassion for the part of us that still hurts—however, we *do* expand into the divine light, because we begin to ask ourselves, "What else could this mean, other than the meaning I've assigned to it?" This allows us to exhibit strength in the midst of what may have once made us feel weak—and that alone is worth it. It's as if we're taking the position of the adult, while they are the child. We can smile down on them and neutralize the wound, so that we no longer unconsciously give away our power.

Empathy and forgiveness can sometimes go hand in hand, but empathy is a portal to many different possi-bilities and helps us to disentangle ourselves from fear, which can keep us stuck in our human story, because we think the bad thing that happened to us back then might happen again if we show compassion. I've heard a lot of people say, "I can't justify what that person did." But that's not what I'm asking here. Too often, we confuse compassion with weakness, but it isn't! The compassion that is born from empathy is precisely what enables us to see into our own blocks and areas of resistance, so that we can be lovingly led to make different decisions and to magnetize experiences that do not (unconsciously) perpetuate the same hurt we experienced in the past.

## Reflection Questions

1. Think of someone in your life you may not be ready to forgive, including yourself. Do you have any fears about offering empathy or compassion to this person? If so, what are they?

2. In thinking of the ways they hurt you, ask, "What else might this mean?" If you were to create some distance from your story of hurt, what starts to become more apparent to you? Take some time to sit with this broader perspective. Notice what changes in your perception of that person, as well as your perception of yourself.

3. How might stepping into your divine light give you the kind of insight that will help you deal with similar situations if they come up in the future?

## IT'S NOT SYMPATHY, EITHER

My husband, Oliver, has many clients that learn his Sacred Geometry Healing Practices who then come to see me to work on other aspects of their healing. Many of them report feeling extremely debilitated in the beginning of their journey before learning from us both. The reason? According to them, "I'm an empath, and it's *so* painful and hard! I just feel people's feelings *all the time,* and it's a *huge* energy drain!"

When I hear this, I nod politely—and I can't help but lovingly call them out. The thing most of them are describing isn't empathy; it's sympathy.

Let me illustrate the difference. When you're sympathizing with someone, you're going out of the bounds of your own soul to be with them and to feel what they're feeling. Because you've vacated your center, you feel shaky, destabilized, not quite like yourself. This is when you're in danger of being drained of your energy—because your boundaries have pretty much gone kaput.

With empathy, you never leave your stable center. You try to understand how the person on the other side feels, but you're also holding it at a safe and appropriate distance. You're not disconnected by any means; rather, you're finally connected to *all* perceptions instead of the disempowering one. In contrast, people who get stuck in sympathy get sucked into the vortex of emotions until they can no longer differentiate between what's theirs and what belongs to someone else. This is understandably debilitating, because it means they're always at the mercy of the emotional shitstorm swirling around them. But this is not necessarily the best way to develop compassion and understanding (in fact, it's a surefire recipe for exactly the opposite, since most "empaths" end up resenting the heck out of the people who drain them). To cultivate empathy, we need more of a bird's-eye view. In other words, empathy takes us above the clouds of the human story and into the beauty, grandeur, and calm of the divine light.

The saying "misery loves company" speaks to the kind of disempowering relationship in which someone agrees to give up their power to join someone else in their lower vibration. This is part of the human story of how we relate to one another while seeking a sense of approval and belonging.

I teach this to practitioners who go through my certification program. They shouldn't get lost in the story of their client or patient, but instead try to understand it holistically and invite the soul they are serving into a place of empowerment. Otherwise, it's like trying to play a video game with the game creators themselves who already know all the cheat codes and twists and turns of the game. You'll never win. (Instead, you can invite them to your space, to your game!) But empathy is not about a desire for approval and belonging. It comes from another place—a perspective of indivisible unity that sees the higher potential of the spirit and recognizes that, on a quantum level, we're always connected and there's a divine reason for this.

One of the things I've come to see is that if we feel debilitated or are caught in a state of compassion fatigue, it means that we have a gift we haven't properly utilized. If we have the ability to feel other people's pain, we can shift our perspective so that we recognize we also have the ability to do something to transmute that pain. Being an "empath" in and of itself is neither a curse nor a blessing; it's all about what we decide to do with it.

Once I began to view my empathy as a gift, I could see and read people's feelings and get a sense of how they'd gotten to where they were. I was not using it to detect danger or protect myself, but as a tool of service. This was something I became known for clinically, and to which I equate a good amount of my success. I can step into someone's mind, understand their thinking patterns without getting lost in their pain and confusion, step out, and serve the person in question to get back on track with their divine story. I've had doctors and scientists shadowing me to try to understand this work! In knowing the full trajectory of their story, I didn't have to simply sit there and say, "Okay, you're right, your life is messed up and sad." Instead, I could fully honor their human story so they felt heard and they knew that I genuinely understood *and* saw the light within them. I could also stay in my own high vibration and maintain a commitment to lovingly inviting them up there with me, instead of going down to keep them company inside the dense forest of their feelings.

Even when I speak at events with thousands of people, I have to check in with myself and ensure that I'm in a state of empathy, which is open and receptive but also empowered. I might tell someone in the crowd who's in the throes of their suffering, "First and foremost, what happened to you wasn't right, *and* I'm here to help you out of it." I want them to feel my genuine compassion without allowing either of us to get lost in their pain. I've realized over the years that isn't what their heart is asking for, anyhow. This is how I can maintain the clarity that helps me steward us into calmer waters.

Remember, this work isn't about "fixing" anyone's problems; it's about lovingly, persistently shining a light on what might be hiding in plain sight, and inviting those around you, of their own volition, to step into that light. As I tell my practitioners, "You are not the giver of information—you are the facilitator of healing."

## Reflection Questions

1. Do you consider yourself an empath? If so, how has this shown up in your life?

2. What do you know about empaths, based on what you've heard and experienced? What are the rewards and drawbacks of being an empath?

3. Are there times you've mistaken sympathy for empathy? How do each of these states feel for you—physically, mentally, and emotionally?

4. When someone you know is in pain, how do you respond—by going "down" into it and taking on their feelings, or inviting them "up" into a higher vibration?

5. How can you practice being a compassionate witness to people's pain by staying in your own power and inviting them to join you in that vibration?

## THE POWER OF SELF-EMPATHY

Empathy isn't just for other people, but it's also for yourself. I often share with my clients and students that starting with showing empathy toward ourselves can be extremely powerful and can even enhance the empathy we demonstrate for others. What we accomplish within us pours out around us.

What we accomplish
within us pours
out around us.

Through self-empathy, we can begin to see all the ways it's hard to have genuine compassion for others because we don't even have it for ourselves. But the divine light gives us insight into the fact that we are all connected. When we villainize other people, it's very likely we're doing the same to ourselves on some level; when we deny the nature of our interconnectedness with others, we lose a sense of connection to ourselves.

A woman at an event years ago explained how terrible her workplace was. She went into great detail about how everyone gossiped and how it was such a toxic environment. I intentionally didn't interrupt her, but instead, I held my high vibration as she continued. After a few minutes, she realized she had been talking for some time, so she stopped and looked at me with shock in her eyes. She was judging everyone for judging everyone! It was a toxic and repetitive cycle. By gently holding space for her, I helped her to come to that conclusion on her own and catch it in real time. And she did so without judging herself for judging others; instead, she released the pattern naturally.

In exercising self-empathy, we move into empowerment. We hold a mirror up to ourselves that helps us to see our own tender hearts—and the many ways and reasons we may have faltered, "screwed up," lost our way, or done things of which we weren't proud. As we shed the light of our own understanding on our actions, we come to see and know ourselves in new ways. We have insights and epiphanies we didn't have before; finally, we start to see a new way, a new path forward. This doesn't come from denial of what we've done but from the willingness to face ourselves and our suffering—to say, "Okay, I see you, and I get why this happened."

When we get really good at empathizing with our own selves (which takes practice, effort, and a gentle attunement to our own experience), we begin to build our fortitude when it comes to empathizing with others.

Many years ago, a very large network asked me to come on one of their shows to speak about trauma. I told them in no uncertain terms, "Yes, I've been through trauma, but I chose some of the experiences that ended up hurting me. I don't think enough folks in the self-development world talk about their own mistakes; I'd like to change that." I ended up not doing the interview, because I didn't want to depict myself as some kind of "pure" person who was the victim of things that had been thrown onto me—and they were not interested in my preferred angle. I wanted people to know that our own choices can be the source of painful wounds at times—and instead of beating ourselves up about this, we can walk a mile in our own moccasins.

At the age of 23, I had an abortion. I deeply regretted the decision and self-punished for years. This manifested in a lot of different ways, including excruciating menstrual cycles. My human story is that I thought I was doing the right thing at the time, especially because I was at the beginning of an abusive relationship. It took me years to truly empathize with and forgive myself . . . to see myself through the eyes of the divine and recognize the limitations in which I'd been working. Feeling worthy of becoming a mom with beautiful children of her own someday was an incredible gift I eventually gave myself, but not without walking through empathy and practicing radical self-forgiveness.

Regret and remorse were absolutely a part of my own journey. Even as I empathized with myself, I did not try to justify my decisions. I wanted to understand why I had made them and be assured that I had learned and evolved. When we love on the human version of ourselves, we automatically step into the light, which has enough room for the complex swirl of feelings and memories that might accompany our most painful experiences.

I've worked with so many people who recognized that self-empathy was a magic potion. One of my old clients confessed that he'd molested his sister when they were children. He'd gone on to build a beautiful life, with a wife and kids he adored, but he continued to loathe himself for what he had done. (You can imagine how in my divine light I needed to be so that my human story and triggers around child abuse weren't activated.) He didn't believe he deserved his happiness and success because of all the pain he'd caused. He came to recognize that, while he still harbored understandable regret over the harm he'd caused, his actions had come from a lack of understanding when he was a child himself—not to mention, from his own sexual trauma.

Together, we discovered that he'd decided the only way he could "pay for" what he'd done was with his own suffering and self-hatred. We often do this to ourselves: attempt to redress the past by sacrificing some part of ourselves in the future. This never works, and it never sets right the wrong that occurred; it only succeeds in perpetuating the energy of shame and self-hatred, which is a low-vibration energy that does not and can never result in healing. What heals us, even if we're dealing with a situation where the person we harmed has not forgiven us, is self-empathy. We can empathize with the version of us that did what it did, and we can start to "pay for our sins" in a totally different way—a beautiful way that is generative and spreads goodness, that allows us to serve the world in a new way (something you'll learn more about in Chapter 5: Transmutation).

Remember Chapter 2 and the whole process of learning to disidentify from events and occurrences, and to recall that our true self is so much bigger than our so-called mistakes? Again, this isn't for the purpose of denying that we did something wrong; it's to take new actions that help us to step into our divine light. In cases like these, we find that our old identity (as a "bad person," a "sinner," or a "screwup," for example) starts to crumble and we come to a new, clear, empowered sense of who we are and who we can be going forward. Instead of paying for our mistakes with shame, we can dedicate ourselves to living a life of service to others. My client who had hurt his sister went on to become a coach, donate his funds to children who'd experienced abuse, and share with his sister what he did and why, which assisted in her own healing. Likewise, as I removed the fear of judgment around my abortion, I was able to share it during events—and without fail, women would come up to me afterward with tears of release in their eyes, as they finally felt they could talk about their own related choices, which they struggled with, sometimes even decades later. Some of these women went on to become the most incredible mothers and some never did, but each of them began their healing journey by going back to the light and into alignment with themselves.

## Reflection Questions

1. Can you stand in empathy with yourself and walk a mile in your own moccasins to understand your actions and behavior? If so, how do you do this? If not, what stops you?

2. In what ways are you still beating yourself up over past mistakes? How does this tend to manifest in your life (e.g., with self-criticism, not being fully present in relationships, depriving yourself of opportunities, etc.)?

3. If you're engaging in self-destructive behavior out of a lack of empathy for yourself, in what ways can you transmute this behavior so that you're actually serving others rather than perpetuating low-vibration energy?

## JUDGMENT AND TAKING PLEASURE IN OTHER PEOPLE'S PAIN

Gossip can traverse the globe in an instant, thanks to social media and the Internet. We've always had some form of tabloid-based gossip that keeps us in a state of self-righteousness, where we don't stop to question the judgments we pass on other people whom we perceive to have messed up in some way—whether they broke a certain social contract or we've deemed them to be "less than" us, usually because of some unspoken rule that our human story created (e.g., "If you want to be rich, you're not a good person—and you should be dragged through the mud for it").

Empathy can feel like such a hurdle when we've been trained to let the arrows of our judgments fly like there's no tomorrow! But our divine light can help us to get clear about our intentions and to break the cycle of *schadenfreude* (a German word that means "pleasure in someone else's misery").

On an energetic level, what's happening when we judge or when we're the ones being judged? I started to ask myself this question as I began working with more celebrity clients and people who were in perceived positions of power. I've had a lot of experience working with a biofeedback machine that maps the frequency of a person's psychic energy, and I've noticed that people who are in the public eye more than the average person tend to have what appears to be excess psychic energy.

This is a clear representation of something that psychology has termed *projection*, which happens when a person redirects feelings that come from their internal ideas about themselves onto someone or something in the external world, as if they were caused by the latter. A good example of this is the following: a person who has been conditioned to believe that expressing their power in any way is bad or negative will see another person who is seemingly more open and accepting of their own power— and then project negative feelings onto that person.

This is why it's not necessarily as easy as it looks to be a famous or well-known person. It's akin to wearing a psychic bodysuit with a Velcro-like surface that picks up all the different projections people fling at you, whether positive or negative. People are literally sitting in your energy field and feeding off you! This causes incredible harm if the celebrity lives predominantly in their human story, and it actually makes them more susceptible to the pain and judgment of being publicly scrutinized.

And if you've done this to someone else, please try to have empathy for yourself. Recognize that the only reason we do this to other people is because it can be an unconscious way of feeling better about ourselves. What we often fail to recognize is that this behavior strips us of our genuine power, even as we are doing it to diminish other people. It can also work in the opposite way: instead of tearing another person down, we might glorify them instead. All of this works in similar ways in that we're typically inserting our own energy into something that appears to have a higher energy than ours. We think we can gain significance or power this way, but we don't.

All gossip and judgment sit in a frequency of "I'm not enough." Instead of facing this frequency directly, we deflect by setting our snares into other people for a momentary dopamine hit that feels like power but really isn't. The judgments we've placed on others typically come from our human story, so by definition they are incomplete. And they often don't even have anything to do with the reality of the situation; rather, our judgments come from meanings we create, based on reference points that have little to nothing to do with that other person.

The energy of judgment tends to drag people down—ourselves and others included—which then leads to further disconnection. But when we start to interrogate our intentions, we can follow the thread of our judgment back to an internal wound or insecurity that offers us insight into how we might be able to nourish ourselves. What is the human need that we're failing to meet and choosing to feed through the energy of judgment?

We all have the capacity to catch ourselves before we take the projections that live inside our shadow and hurl them onto others. In doing so, we can access a higher realm that helps us to meet our needs and doesn't work to generate a false sense of reality—which is very much the terrain of all the fear-mongering we see on social media and the news. This comes from the parts of the self that have not evolved enough to understand that they can access unlimited energy in a totally different way. This energy is bountiful, but to play with it, we must learn to raise our consciousness.

The trick isn't "judging the judger," as we've already learned. It's pausing long enough to have empathy with the part of us that's attempting to get its need for energy and power met, but in an unskillful way. In this way, we use empathy to shed light on our judgments and to take our projections back so that we can powwow in the domain of the divine.

## Reflection Questions

1. Think of the last person you had a huge judgment about. What was the human need you were trying to meet in judging them? Was it to feel connected to a group of people with the same judgment? To avoid the behavior that the other person was displaying? To feel better about yourself? (Please be very honest and gentle with yourself.)

2. In what ways do your judgments keep you from seeing the big picture and distract you from playing full out in your own divine light?

3. The next time a similar judgment comes up, how might you try to redirect it so that you aren't flinging your projections onto someone else but choosing to meet the human need that's connected to the judgment?

## THE TRAP OF "I'M NOT LIKE THAT"

One of the things that can keep us stuck in our projections onto other people is our sense of righteous indignation—especially if we're judging someone who's committed heinous crimes or behaved in ways that are detrimental to others. I do believe there's a place for this anger, which can absolutely be transmuted into conscious and empowering action from a place of care, love, and dedication to higher values. However, we can inadvertently back ourselves into a corner when we operate on the misconception that "the only people I judge do bad (or heinous) things—things I'd never do in a million years!"

Of course, that might be true on a superficial level. You might have an ax to grind when it comes to people who verbally and physically abuse their children, but it's possible that you haven't taken the time to look deeply at another behavior you have that might make your own child feel unloved. Sure, it might sound like we're comparing apples to oranges—but the point is, every single one of us has the potential to act out of alignment with our higher self. The way that looks will vary from person to person, but what we often judge in another is a part of our own self that we've shoved into the shadows without taking the time to look at it with empathy.

I think about this concept a lot when I encounter people who hold on to the abuse that someone inflicted on them when they were younger. They may be rightfully angry and upset about what occurred, but sometimes, unconsciously, they internalize some aspect of the abuser because they haven't learned to let it go. This can be apparent with folks with dissociative identity disorder, where some of their fractured personalities present as an "inner abuser."

I also think of someone I know well, who suffers from mental illness. She also had a deeply traumatic childhood that was full of the most awful abuse. During the times when she'd hurt her child, she'd insist, "I'm not a monster!" Unfortunately, her actions said otherwise. My observation of her was that she'd unconsciously carried around the pain of what had happened to her, and because she struggled with staying in a conscious and emotionally aware state long enough to work through it, she ricocheted between victim and perpetrator. The energy of the abuse was still locked into her system, and even though she firmly believed that she wasn't an abuser, she'd unconsciously absorbed many of the same behaviors that had harmed her so greatly when she was young.

Another way of looking at this is: Have you ever noticed that people who absolutely swear they'll never end up like their parents usually end up perpetuating a behavior that's the same as or similar to the very thing they said they'd never do?

Empathy can help us to see that while each of us has our own unique path, we're not actually all that different from each other. We all contain aspects of shadow and light—and to paraphrase a common spiritual idea: The more we resist seeing in ourselves what we project onto others, the more it persists—often, without our conscious awareness. And every time we are triggered, the unhealed part of the self crashes the party and has the potential to wreak havoc and drag us into the darkness.

Questioning "I'm not like that" can free us from our judgments and stretch our hearts and minds open. Earlier in the book, I mentioned the well-known saying, "Hurt people hurt people." This is true for us, too, if we let it be. We may hurt others directly; or perhaps, by not shining our light, we rob the world of the opportunity to experience the wonderful whole version of us. The more we lovingly embrace the parts of ourselves that have been bruised, beaten, and battered by our experiences, the likelier we are to reclaim our power so that we don't start leaking our energy in unskillful ways.

## Reflection Questions

1. Can you identify someone you feel triggered by, whose behavior is 180 degrees from yours?

2. Take a step back and allow yourself to expand into your divine light. Ask yourself: *In what ways am I not as different from this person as I've made myself believe?* List the ways you've displayed similar behaviors. (This may be a hard one if you've selected an individual who holds a lot of darkness, but do your best. Or use someone who's a bit easier to start this process with.)

3. In lovingly, empathetically taking back your projections onto this person, how are you taking back your power and your ability to make different decisions going forward?

## RELEASING TOXIC ENERGETIC HOLDS

As we explored in the last two sections, exercising empathy helps us to become clear about the ways we've unconsciously given our power away—through our projections and judgments.

During one of my talks, I shared thoughts about forgiveness and empathy. Someone in the audience shared this breakthrough observation: "Empathy became necessary in releasing myself from the energetic hold another person or experience had on me."

That sentiment sums up one of the most important reasons for exercising empathy: it allows us to move forward by releasing the energetic shackles that have kept us in place. Sometimes, these shackles are there without anyone's knowledge. Other times, they're present because someone or something has been actively trying to gain energy from us. Consider the energy of someone who is an abuser or manipulator—who is consciously attempting to exert control over someone else to gain power. Sadly, there are too many people out there who are wrangling for power because they think it's a limited resource. (Of course, this is never true when we're living inside the light, which doesn't require stripping someone of their power to feel our own.)

Our empathy can help us to separate from the toxic hold that someone else might have over us because we've chosen to obsess over that person or unconsciously allow them to inhabit some part of our life without our full awareness or consent.

I've been raped twice, by people whom I believed were my friends. When I told my husband about it, he was bewildered by my language. "Mandy . . . do you realize that's the definition of rape?" he asked, his voice and facial expression full of compassion. I was shocked. I hadn't defined the incidents as *rape* because I had such an aversion to feeling like a victim—to the extent that I believed admitting that I was raped was a form of self-victimization!

Oliver gently inquired as to who these men were. Much to our chagrin, we discovered that I still had their contact information in my phone, even though I hadn't talked to them in years. Sadly, this is not uncommon. Many people who have been raped might maintain some kind of connection with their perpetrator because, in a strange way, the connection keeps them from admitting to the abuse. There was a part of me that didn't want to fully face what had happened, so keeping these men in my life was also an unconscious way of delaying the healing process.

As I stood in empathy with my own experience, without shame or self-loathing, I realized that it was time to cut these men out of my life once and for all. I knew that the energetic connection would only continue to feed the wound and possibly ensure that I keep reliving it to a certain extent—until I could finally understand what had happened and release it for good.

It was time to close the loop. I didn't have to keep replaying the old stories. And yes, I could even have empathy for these men, who had acted in such base and misguided ways. So often, we think that holding on to anger or resentment toward people who've hurt us will prevent future terrible experiences. This is an understandable protection mechanism, but it's a limited version of the truth. Empathy launches us into a state of neutrality that helps us refocus our energy on actually healing.

Empathy launches
us into a state of
neutrality that helps
us refocus our energy
on actually healing.

In my case, I had to heal my perception of not believing I was enough, which had kept me from acknowledging the reality of what had happened to me, since I'd been so terrified of feeling like a victim. I could finally close the loop—ensuring that the people who had hurt me, as well as my memory of those experiences, would no longer continue to drain my energy.

One thing I truly, deeply believe is that the greatest revenge is a beautiful life. Empathy is a skill that keeps us connected to the light within and that allows us to neutralize any unconscious feelings or energetic connections that have kept us from healing.

## Reflection Questions

1. Can you think of an experience you haven't fully released? How does this experience continue to take up space in your heart, mind, and body? The point of this question is not to relive a trauma, so skip this question if it triggers excessive pain.

2. What belief was birthed from the thing that happened to you? (In my case, it was "It's a bad thing to be a victim, so I'm going to cover this up and not acknowledge that it happened.")

3. How can being in empathy with your experience help you to see clearly, close the loop, and get free from the toxic energetic hold the experience may still have over you?

4. How can empathizing with the person or people who harmed you neutralize your connection to them and help you take your power back?

## TAKE YOUR JUDGMENTS BACK

One thing I really want to reemphasize about empathy is that it helps us to neutralize emotionally charged experiences and to take our power back. If there's anything I want you to get from this chapter, it's that this is one of the most powerful reasons to exercise empathy. Unfortunately, many of us believe that empathy actually strips us of whatever power we have; out of pride, we tell ourselves, "This person doesn't deserve my empathy!" We cast them (and in some cases, ourselves) in the role of villain, as we attempt to assert our power through harsh and heavy judgments.

However, this isn't true power. True power exists in the light, which casts itself lovingly on the bigger picture behind people's wounded actions and behaviors, and holds them in a space of neutrality and love. This doesn't mean we justify all actions, or allow just anyone into our lives, but being able to see the big picture is what frees us.

I saw this when I began examining my judgments of a woman I know quite well who had made some terrible choices during her previous marriage. I felt that the ways she'd behaved toward her ex-husband and child were disgusting and unconscionable. I felt perfectly justified in my judgments. I slowly began putting the pieces together and realized that my anger was fuel that would help me to fight her to protect her ex-husband and child. I felt harboring this judgment helped me to stay strong and determined, so I could do what needed to be done to help the victims in the situation. Eventually, I found love in my heart for this woman and genuinely empathized with her. This couldn't really happen until I was able to ensure that the people she'd hurt were safely out of her reach—then and only then could I refocus my attention and energy on empathy for her. (I always say that if you or someone you love is in danger, your foremost responsibility is to find safety.)

Judgment can help us to serve our own intentions and purpose—it's certainly appropriate when the well-being of a child is at risk—but outside of that, there are far better ways to blow off steam than talking poorly about another person and sending out negative energy we'll only end up bringing back on ourselves. Judgment occupies a very limiting, dark, and claustrophobic space inside the human story, even though we have tons of justifications for it. But we can learn to transmute our judgments, so they become catalysts for positive change. In my case, "Gosh, how could someone be so terrible?" shifted into "I love these people so much, and I want to keep them safe." The focus on my positive intention also enabled me to extend more grace to this woman who was obviously in so much pain, and I was eventually able to help her (she even asked for it!).

The temptation to talk poorly about others is fed and fueled by our gossip-hungry society. There's a story in my family about my great-grandmother, who was a wonderful teacher in her own right. She strongly disliked speaking negatively about anyone else, even if it seemed justified. Once, at a get-together with other women in her neighborhood, everyone took turns speaking ill of a man who'd cheated on his wife. When it was my grandmother's turn, all she had to say was, "Well, he sure can whistle." It was a hilarious moment. Not exactly the greatest compliment—but she operated on the premise that if you can't say anything nice, it's best not to say anything at all!

The bottom line is: we need not invite our consciousness into the hurt parts of people, especially in instances when we can't do anything about the situation and it's not our place to judge. And if we *can* do something? Then, we don't waste our sentiments on tongue lashings or sending negative energy; instead, we roll up our sleeves and take action in service of improving the situation.

*Monsters, Inc.* is an animated film in which a group of monsters feed off the energy of fear by sneaking into the bedrooms of children and scaring them. The screams of the frightened children are then captured and used as an energy source. At the end of the movie (spoiler alert if you haven't seen it!), the main characters realize that laughter is a far more powerful energy source than fear— so they decide to dedicate themselves to making children laugh instead of scaring them. This is kind of how judgment works: it may give us a temporary form of power, but over time, it only ends up draining us. When we tap into the divine light through empathy, we tap into a vast and infinite wellspring of power that feeds not just us, but the world around us.

## PRACTICE: TAKE YOUR JUDGMENTS BACK

1.  Think of a major judgment that you hold against a person, a group, or a situation. (You can do this on a very personal or a very global level; in fact, it can be helpful to do this exercise for more than one judgment!)

2.  What is the need you are attempting to meet through this judgment? Don't judge yourself as you evaluate this, or fall into self-labeling. Simply identify what's behind it. For example, perhaps the judgment meets your need for significance. Maybe it makes you feel like you're a good person because it gives you a reminder of how you can stay in your own integrity instead of making the same mistake.

3.  Is there a better way to go about getting this need met that doesn't zap you of your own power and energy? For example, maybe creating a beautiful piece of art, or connecting with a loved one (be mindful of the times when "connection" looks like gossip or negativity, though, as this is another unhealthy way of meeting a basic need).

4.  Now that you've been able to give yourself constructive empathy, start a process of inquiry about the person you're judging. What is your judgment? For example, maybe you believe that your ex should have given you more love and failed to.

5.  What is the proof that this person acted badly toward you or others? Again, this isn't about making yourself wrong, but about expanding the scope of your perception. Do you know the other person's full story? Is there anything about their past that might explain their poor treatment of you or anyone else? Is it possible that the meaning you've placed on this experience is incomplete?

6. Remind yourself that if you experienced hurt at someone else's hands, that's never okay. But instead of being stuck in that hurt, let yourself neutralize it. You might wish to say to yourself, "I'm willing to see and be supported by a larger story, and to understand why things went the way they went. Any feelings of shame, bitterness, resentment, and judgment are now being neutralized. This no longer has control over me, and I'm willing to move through it."

## YOUR DIVINE LIGHT PRACTICE

Repeat the *Take Your Judgments Back* practice. You can work with one or several strong judgments, but work with only one at a time. Just like the last practice in Chapter 2, this can be a wonderful exercise for learning to meet our human needs in a more powerful way. It can also help us to step into empathy as a natural response over time.

As always, take time to revisit the reflection questions at the end of each section in this chapter, and to journal on them.

## Takeaways

1. The simple question, "What else could this mean?" can help us open up to the energy of the third pathway of light, **empathy**, which expands our awareness of the story we've been telling ourselves about the hurt someone has caused us.

2. Empathy is not the same thing as forgiveness or condoning someone else's bad behavior. However, empathy can broaden our perspective and help us to let go of our limited human interpretations so that we can get a glimpse of the bigger picture, which gives us a greater sense of understanding and compassion.

3. Whereas sympathy can feel destabilizing and shake us out of our center so that we start absorbing other people's emotional states, empathy always allows us to stay centered, neutral, and in our power.

4. Often, the person who most needs our empathy is us! Standing in empathy with ourselves can help us to see our lives with greater perspective, and to act in ways that are beneficial to us and others instead of continuing to beat ourselves up over our perceived mistakes.

5. One of the great killers of empathy is judgment, which can give us a sense of momentary power but only ends up draining us in the long term.

6. When we start to own our projections instead of insisting, "I could never do the terrible thing that other person did," we deactivate the unconscious power such projections have over us. We also learn to own the parts of ourselves that might be hiding an inner perpetrator.

7. Empathy is one of the best ways to take our power back and to release the toxic energetic hold that a memory, person, or situation has over us.

8. Removing strong judgments from ourselves and others can open us up to empathy and help us to meet our needs in a higher-vibration way.

# CHAPTER 4

# clarity

Basking in the divine light is similar to seeing a beautiful work of art that is so vast and all-encompassing, we have to step back to truly drink it in and appreciate it . . . to really even *see* it. Appreciating the divine is an aesthetic experience that touches all our senses and our capacity for **clarity**, which is the fourth pathway of light. And clarity isn't just a crisp picture—it's our ability to hold the complexity of our experience with awe and wonder, to see and know the truth, and to make decisions that honor us and the people around us. Clarity helps us to reach a sense of understanding with a clear, undiluted vision that isn't distorted by our human wants and needs. The clarity I'm talking about invites us to recognize and welcome a range of different emotional frequencies, and to be moved and humbled to our core by what is available when we act from integrity, authenticity, and truth.

I got a great lesson in clarity when I met my bonus son, who came into my life when he was four, after I got into a relationship with Oliver. He was such a bright light: smart, funny, sweet, and so soulful. I loved that he had such a strong, healthy, secure connection with his dad. However, I could sense that he didn't have the same kind of healthy attachment with women. The first night I met him, we all did a prayer together. I can still remember what he said, verbatim: "Dear God, thank you for Mandy, thank you for Mandy, thank you for Mandy." I knew in that moment that this kid was going to have my heart. Like so many children, he was touchingly honest and expressive about his love from the get-go, and it melted me. At the same time, I could sense that his rapid attachment to me was due to the fact that he didn't have many strong connections with women.

As time passed, I did everything to make sure that my son was absolutely taken care of in every possible way, especially as I came to learn more about the traumas he'd faced from an early age, as his parents had had a difficult marriage. I was heartbroken to learn about everything this beautiful young soul had been put through at such a tender age.

Of course, I became a Mama Bear who wanted to protect him at all costs and keep him from experiencing any further trauma. I was also pretty aggressive about it. I was angry at some of what he had had to go through, which tugged at my own childhood wounds. I did all I could to contribute to his healing. I made sure he got therapy, and I poured all my energy and resources into ensuring he would be functional, happy, and healthy—and that he'd grow up to have great relationships rather than continuing to carry the legacy of the wounding he had experienced. In many ways, it worked. Today, he is a deeply conscious and aware young man, and he's healed so much. He is also no longer in the situations from which I worked so hard to remove him.

However, as he began to grow up, I had the epiphany that everything I'd done to protect him was no longer working—and that Mama Bear was no longer my role to play. I was starting to see that he was now at an age where he needed to learn to stand on his own two feet. It was so clear to me that I was actually supposed to take a step back. Of course, there was a part of me that was writhing in resistance at the mere idea, since I'm hardwired to help people get free from pain. However, as lots of parents ultimately discover, there are times when we have to let go and recognize that our children are radiant souls on their own journey. My son had things he needed to learn on his own, without me shadowing his every step to make sure he didn't experience pain. In fact, it became so clear to me that the most loving thing I could do was give him the freedom to stretch and grow into the man he would become, with all the lessons that were his to learn and integrate.

I'd come to discern something really important (discernment is a huge part of clarity): what had worked for him at an early age was quickly becoming obsolete. I was starting to feel that my old protective stance had become quite heavy, for both me and my son. It was taking on a more controlling frequency, which didn't feel good to me. And so, the shift began. I became more discerning about the times when it was right and necessary, and when it was better for me to step back so he could gather the skills to care for himself and learn his own soulful lessons. This would require him to sit with his emotions (which is a huge aspect of this chapter) so that he could gain an understanding of how to move himself forward. I would always do what was in my power to point him in the direction of light so he could have the most amazing and beautiful life available to him. But I refused to hinder him in any way. By stepping back and retracting that protective Mama Bear energy, I could let him "fail forward" and figure things out on his own.

As I stepped further into clarity, I also realized that staying in a space of "this is right or wrong," and villainizing anyone I perceived had hurt someone else (even in minor ways), meant I was stuck in my human story. The people I saw as villains were actually some of my greatest teachers, and they were unknowingly inviting me to see through my soul's eyes. I had forgotten that hurt people hurt people, while whole people help people. It's a tall order to ask someone who has been hurt never to inflict any hurt themselves, and I was holding people to standards I myself couldn't fully elevate to. I was being called to become more whole myself, to address this particular pattern from my elevated self. I realized that, similarly to generational trauma, patterns only continue until someone elevates and breaks the chain. I was being called to do just that.

I saw myself in another reality, shaking hands with the higher self of anyone I met (including my son, as well as the people I felt had hurt him) as we each agreed to learn some of the hardest and most beautiful lessons of this lifetime. My son, myself, and anyone else who came into my life in some way were all souls on our own personal journeys. As I worked on expanding the clarity of what else was available in various situations, it was impossible not to find love and understanding. And since love is my nature, it gave me the courage to break the pattern by practicing compassion and exercising clarity whenever I felt tunnel vision closing in on me. Yes, we had all experienced pain, and at times, we got hurt—but the greater clarity of my perception was that we are not what happened to us; we are who we were before we even got here: light. In other words, my son was light! And so were the people I believed had inflicted harm on him.

The results have been nothing short of wonderful. That's not to say that things are perfect, as my son is still a kid who's learning more about himself and the world—and challenges are part of the process! However, in seeing the way he is showing up in the world and for himself, I am deeply proud of him. Even through his stumbling blocks, it's evident that he's learning to embody his light in ways that are particular to his experience and life stage. I don't know exactly how any of this will play out for him, but at the very least, I know he'll be empowered and capable of handling whatever life sends his way with grace and strength. And another thing I'm so clear about is that my love will always be here, as I watch from an appropriate distance and clearly see the beautiful person he continues to grow into.

## TRUTH IS WHAT'S IN THE HIGHEST GOOD

As I discovered in parenting my son, clarity is about embracing truth, which is always in the highest good of everyone involved. Truth-tellers are spiritual warriors who shine the light on what is possible when we stand in our soul (which I'll share more about in Chapter 5). And standing in clarity is all about standing in the vibration of truth, which is always in the highest good of everyone involved, even when it doesn't look or feel like it at first glance.

Tough love is always about the truth, which I discovered for myself when I contemplated my evolving role in my son's life—but I want to be clear about something: choosing truth *never* causes pain! It is always in the highest good.

Our skewed perceptions can sometimes cause us to believe that living in our authenticity is hard, or that it has the potential to hurt someone. In addition, it is the fact that we chose fear to begin with that eventually ends up hurting people. For example, I once had a boyfriend whom I decided to leave because the dynamics of our relationship were toxic for us both. I realized that I'd chosen a relationship in which I didn't love the other person 100 percent, which was perhaps a reason the connection became toxic and abusive. I'd made poor decisions from fear, which had caused me to stay with him for so long. Over time, fear like this compounds and creates a storm in our life.

As soon as we move into truth, it's not as if the lives of the people around us are suddenly destroyed (and if that's the case, we probably chose selfishness over love!). Most often, as we begin clearing the clutter of our out-of-alignment decisions, we and the people around us experience healing. It's like breaking a bone to set it in its proper place.

Today, I know there's no decision I can make from truth that would end up diminishing or greatly hurting anyone. The greatest act of love is to unflinchingly stand in the clear light of truth, which allows us to move toward harmony and clarity.

The greatest
act of love is to
unflinchingly stand
in the clear light of
truth, which allows
us to move toward
harmony and clarity.

My mother decided to leave my stepfather after she learned about some of his addictive behaviors that had led him to make poor and hurtful decisions. When she finally left, she wondered how the divorce would affect me and my siblings. As I mentioned earlier, I couldn't have been happier for her, especially since I'd never seen a whole version of her inside that relationship.

Mom said, "I'm really worried that he'll fall apart . . . that he won't survive without me."

I posed a question to her: "What if he'll thrive without you?" She was shocked by the notion, which she hadn't considered.

After their divorce, my stepfather went through a rough time that included homelessness, which was difficult for our family. While I no longer speak with him, I'm aware that he eventually turned his life around. He hasn't had a drink in years, and he currently works as a manager at a halfway house, helping others to get clean. My mother could never have "saved" him inside their marriage—making yourself miserable by being afraid of hurting someone else won't stop them from being who they are! But her decision to release the relationship allowed him to become the version of himself that he needed to become.

This makes me think of the relationship I left behind. Although my boyfriend admitted that he'd take whatever scraps I could throw his way because he was so afraid of me leaving, I knew that it was more loving to let go because he deserved to be loved fully. Facing the truth allows us to recognize that the perceived unconscious rewards of whatever we're experiencing (in this case, my boyfriend's sense that he'd settle for being unloved because it was preferable to being alone) are but a shadow of what we could have if we stepped fully into the light of clarity.

I want to explore this idea of perceived unconscious rewards in more depth. Although it can be hard to accept at first, it's often operating in some way or shape in our lives, even though we're seldom aware of it (that's why they're unconscious!). Let's look at something in your life that makes you unhappy that has been persistently present. Let's say you're in a toxic relationship with a partner, a parent, a boss, or someone else. Ultimately, no human being does anything they don't want to do, and even when we're in pain, we're getting exactly what we want—albeit, a diminished version of whatever we think is worth holding on to such relationships. Maybe that thing is connection, or familiarity, or comfort, or simply a means to put food on the table. For some reason, we haven't considered that something better, something that honors our wholeness, will come if we are willing to let go.

When we come into a state of clarity, we start to understand the perceived and unconscious rewards that live inside our most painful choices—which is why we lovingly move in the direction of being conscious of what we're asking for, and why.

This might sound callous to someone who has, say, been in a string of abusive relationships, but I want to explain why this approach is transformative when seen through the eyes of clarity. Before I met Oliver, I tended to attract abusive relationships. My human story was about my victimization, but when I stretched into the light, I recognized that some part of me was actually thrilled that my partners were emotionally unavailable, because that activated my trauma response and allowed me to always keep one foot out the door. The reward, in this case, was that I never had to truly risk being vulnerable.

When we view our patterns with loving emotional honesty, we actually stop wallowing in shame or self-pity. Instead, we assume compassionate responsibility and get clear about why we would choose pain for ourselves. We also give ourselves genuine empathy, as well as the opportunity to make different choices (and I did, which led to meeting my amazing husband). The reason truth is so important in this process is that it's the only thing that is capable of healing our deep-seated shame so we can claim more of our divinity.

When I come across people who are, let's say, afraid to leave toxic relationships or make dramatic decisions because they fear that they'll hurt themselves or the people involved, I often ask them to expand their perspective by asking themselves the question, "If I stay, what will life look like 10, 20, or 30 years down the road?"

The energy and vibration of obligation are extremely low—to the extent that they're very close to the frequency of death. Obligatory energy vacillates in the space of "maybe," and there's no place quite as excruciating as limbo. Sometimes we avoid making a decision to maintain the status quo, or we do something impulsive from fear. Clarity is the frequency of ultimate truth, and when we fearlessly face it, we take the path of least resistance. When we do not, this creates an energetic ball and chain that will drag us down and make it more difficult to recognize the light that's waiting to welcome us back home to our wholeness.

## Reflection Questions

1.  Have there been times when you avoided facing the truth because you were afraid of hurting someone? How did that experience turn out? If you ultimately left that situation, what helped you to move into greater clarity?

2.  If you need a reality check about something painful that you're currently facing, ask yourself, "If I stay in this situation for the next 5 (10, 15, 20 . . . ) years, what will my life look like?"

3.  Then ask yourself, "If I speak my truth today, what will my life look like 5 (10, 15, 20 . . . ) years from now?"

## WHEN WE GET STUCK AND CAN'T SEE CLEARLY

The process of getting to clarity is as holy and mysterious as the divine itself. Through a purely human lens, it isn't always necessarily easy, but there are certainly things we do that make it harder than it has to be.

I remember meeting a woman named Lisa at one of my retreats. She was stuck in a difficult human story, as her husband had fallen ill from cancer and died in a way that was very slow, sad, and painful. "I live in a constant state of unhappiness because I feel so guilty," she admitted. Lisa's two sisters-in-law felt she could have done more to help her husband, even though there was actually very little she could have done. As she told her story, she continued to repeat herself through her sobs. It was clear that she had continued to spin out at the question of whether she could have done more for her husband.

With deep compassion and love, I asked, "Do you see how this experience has become a part of you?" It had been a couple of years since her husband had died—enough time to experience a fuller range of emotions instead of her constant, incessant feeling of paralyzing guilt. "Do you see you're experiencing the pain connected to the perception of who you were when you lost him?" I tried to show her that her guilt and regret were artifacts of that painful time, like a record doomed to just keep repeating. As we tend to do with most traumatic events, she'd been frozen in the experience, without a way out.

However, Lisa couldn't seem to hear me. She continued to bawl and repeat herself—to insist on the veracity of her feelings. She was so stuck that nothing I said seemed to help. "I have no doubt that what you're feeling is very genuine to you, Lisa," I gently explained, "but when you recycle these experiences of grief, trauma, and guilt, you might be forgetting there are probably times when you actually don't feel these feelings. Would you say that's accurate?"

She considered this. "Yes, but it's so rare."

I told her there was another version of herself that was available and asked for permission to lovingly interrupt her every time she recounted the story from a less-than-empowered place. "This is so you can see both the way you choose to revert into that story, and also the way you're not actually in it all the time." We agreed that I would say the word *bananas* whenever Lisa slipped back into her story of excruciating guilt. Sure enough, as she continued, I loudly interjected: "Bananas!" At first, Lisa looked at me like I was weird and continued. I said, "Bananas!" a few more times, until she was thoroughly frustrated with me. But I continued to lovingly but persistently hold her in the light; I would simply not allow her to fully retreat back into the dark depths she had grown so comfortable with and so addicted to.

"Are you starting to see how you're going into that space of darkness by choice?" I asked.

Lisa began to realize that her stuckness was, in fact, a choice. She sighed. "I know there are things that happen that bring me back into sadness, but I also realize this is something I'm actually choosing. And I understand I've chosen it for reasons that seem wonderful and loving on the surface. I want to be a good person, but I also see that I've made this choice unconsciously to punish myself so that I can feel as bad as my husband felt." As we gained more clarity about what was happening, it became obvious that the feelings of guilt weren't as "real" as she'd thought. There was an unhealed part of her that was running the show.

I made it very clear to Lisa that I understood. I knew from my own experience of grieving Eliana that if I'd taken on the role of "grieving mother," I would have received validation in spades! People would have felt sorry for me, and I would have been able to feed off their energy. I've witnessed many people fall into this choice—whether consciously or not. When we're given these massive opportunities to step into the light, we can end up throwing sticks into the spokes of the wheel that was promising to take us toward the blessings.

This is why I often emphasize that even when we're in the midst of excruciating pain, it's always our choice as to whether or not we'll stay stuck. We gain clarity when we begin to interrogate the reasons we're stuck. We start to poke holes in our own reasons for why we can't climb out of the dark hole. We begin recognizing all the places where we've professed loyalty to an extremely limiting human story—because that's what it means to be a "good person," or that's how we believe we can honor the memory of a loved one, or whatever our excuse might be.

Many of us get stuck inside that dark hole, feeling like we aren't strong enough to come out of it. The grieving process isn't linear and tends to come in waves. But when the waves feel more like a constant onrush, and our story becomes a whirlpool that drowns us, we can start to gain clarity that we are not in the midst of a healthy grieving process. Grief is supposed to open up the channels to blocked emotions; it is not meant to be debilitating or to give us an excuse to wallow in a disempowering story that causes us to turn against our own self.

Grief is a beautiful and healthy process, and while it may take a long time to get through, it is not meant to hold us underwater for long, immersive stretches. With clarity, we can lovingly say, "I understand this is a very real emotion. It sucks and it's painful, and while I'm willing to move through it, I'm not willing to stay stuck. I want to see if there's another reality that also has healing or peace or understanding readily available to me."

It takes a lot of courage to recognize it's okay to leave the pain behind. Sometimes, we mistakenly believe that we need to be loyal to our pain by holding on to it. But pain is just an indication of the places within ourselves where transformation is yearning to happen—where our limited human story is ready to expand into the loving and limitless light of the divine. That divine light is large enough to hold our pain, but it will always serve to point us in the direction of high-vibration expressions of joy and beauty. We're meant to experience the full spectrum of life on this earth—but when we get caught in one frequency or the other, we lose out on the opportunity to behold the entire glorious panorama and say, "Wow!"

My client Maria basically came to me half alive. Her soul was so far from her eyes that she looked dead; she could barely formulate a sentence and spoke in a dull, cold monotone. She had lost her son and her husband suddenly— one right after the other. The trauma had almost consumed her. But amazingly, because she used the tools I presented and remained open to the ways I challenged her beliefs and ideas about loss, her turnaround was rapid. Within a year, the light had returned to her eyes. She still experienced pain, but in her words, "I'm able to observe myself whenever my human stuff comes up, and I can easily love myself through the experience." Maria has become devoted to serving others who are stuck in disempowering tunnel vision.

When Maria's second son almost died in the same way as her first son, she messaged me and told me how different everything feels now. "I didn't fall apart," she said. "I focused on doing healings on my son, and he recovered miraculously." I know that her capacity to see clearly— through the lens of a divine story infused with light and pure knowing—is what helped her to outgrow the role of the grieving wife and mother. Now, the woman I get to witness is the exact opposite of the sad and vacant person who came to me in search of her lost soul. She tells me that she's more alive, more embodied, and more clear about her purpose than she's ever been before.

**Reflection Questions**

1.  What disempowering story do you find yourself telling again and again? Why do you think that is? What do you get out of your stuckness?

2.  Are there any recurring disempowering emotions that you tend to get stuck inside? Is there a repeating theme in your life that you may have inherited from a parent or someone else? What kinds of emotions might you be keeping yourself from experiencing because of your loyalty to a disempowering story?

3.  Can you acknowledge that your disempowering story is not the full story? Can you begin to open up to a different reality—and a different way of understanding and perceiving yourself and your life? Most of all, can you engage in these reflections with deep love and from a neutral place?

## LET YOUR YOKE BE EASY AND YOUR BURDEN LIGHT

Clarity connects us to a frequency of ease, because it's about acting from authenticity and integrity. Many of us are raised with the notion that to be a "good" person, we must stay in situations that deplete our energy and cause us to compartmentalize larger aspects of ourselves. When we stay in situations out of obligation, this can take us further from our light. Lisa felt obligated to carry the burden of guilt, which caused her to vibrate in a state of paralyzing fear and anguish.

Often, I'll ask people who are clearly remaining in a bad situation out of guilt, "Would you be okay with what you're doing if it were your child experiencing this instead of you?" Their response reveals vital information about whether or not they're making the right decision. So does the frequency of the decision itself. If it comes from a place of fear, we know it's time to shift into divine love and truth.

Pierre came to one of my masterminds, and he was grappling with the fact that his parents were getting older and their health was rapidly declining. He felt lost in a sea of obligations, but he also had resistance to the idea that, as the oldest son, he should be the one to step up and take care of them. This was because he carried considerable family trauma. His parents had never been accepting or kind toward him. Pierre was a deeply creative soul who had created an oasis that was antithetical to his upbringing. "I'm different from my family, and they've never appreciated or tolerated that," he told me. Although he was carrying a lot of static from decades of unresolved hurt, he flew from his home in Costa Rica to his parents' home in California to take care of them. He was currently considering moving closer to them to be their primary caregiver.

I inquired, "Does that feel good to you?"

He sighed and said, "No, of course not. But I'm their son and it's my duty."

I fully understood that Pierre, like many of us, had been indoctrinated with the idea that it's a child's duty to suck it up and be there for their parents in their time of need. This is usually accompanied by a sense of guilt that sounds like, "They took care of me when I was young, so I need to do the same."

I said, "I would never tell you what to do, but here's what I will offer if you choose to accept. For the next two weeks, you're not allowed to do anything or make any decisions that feel vibrationally heavy. And trust me, you'll know what that feels like without me having to describe it." This was an assignment I gave everyone in my mastermind—and let me tell you, the results were incredible.

Pierre didn't go to his parents' house when he arrived in California, because he recognized that the energy behind this decision was extremely heavy. As he contemplated his situation with a greater sense of clarity, he came to understand, "I want my decisions to come from a place of love, and I realized that what I was doing was not about love. It was about the feeling that I owed them something. Society told me this is what I had to do in order to be a good son, but I don't owe my parents anything."

Pierre's willingness to go through with the exercise was life-changing for him. He sent a beautiful letter to his parents explaining his decision. Although they didn't understand or accept his reasons (which was aligned with the energy they'd doused him with all his life), he felt lighter and more free—which is how he knew it was the right decision.

One way to get clear about whether your decisions are aligned with the highest good is to consider how you feel when you're making them. Do you feel heavy, or do you feel light? Heaviness can feel a lot like being stuck in your head, or having a crushing weight over your heart. Things might look good on the surface, but they don't feel good deep inside. In contrast, when you feel light, you shift to the frequency of the heart. (In fact, moving into good decisions necessitates dropping from the head to the heart, as you've probably already guessed!) You operate from authenticity, ease, and truth, even if your decisions make little sense to anyone but you.

When we move into lightness, we move into the light—and life begins to unfold with greater beauty and ease. Like Pierre experienced, we reconnect with the quantum field of pure potential and possibility. We no longer choose to live in fear or make space for a crappy reality that drags us and everyone else down.

Months later, Pierre got in contact with me. He was back in Costa Rica. "I just keep thinking of how great I felt when I wrote that letter to my parents and finally spoke my truth," he said. "I intentionally poured so much love and honesty into it. I also realized it wouldn't feel 'light' for me to completely abandon them, so I asked my siblings for help in reorganizing their schedules so that my parents would be taken care of."

Pierre's capacity to step out of the cycle of toxicity, which would have continued had he gone along with the notion of what he thought it took to be a "good son," would have been detrimental to everyone—his parents, his siblings, himself—involved. He laid the pain of the past to rest by making a clear and informed choice that literally and figuratively lightened his energetic burden. Pierre understood that the healing journey doesn't have to be delayed for a future "more convenient" time. It can happen in the moment that counts the most: right now.

## Reflection Questions

1.  Is there anything in your life that you're doing out of obligation rather than love? What is the cost of carrying the burden of obligation?

2.  Consider what the sensations of heaviness and lightness feel like in your body. Contemplate the last decision that made you feel heavy, as well as the last decision that led to a feeling of lightness. Where did each of these decisions take you?

3.  For the next two weeks, can you commit to making only decisions that lead to a feeling of lightness? If not, what is the source of your resistance?

## FINDING CLARITY BY FEELING EVERYTHING

If it isn't obvious by now, clarity isn't just about seeing something with laser precision. It's about seeing and feeling *everything* in all its dimensions and textures. Yes, it will include sadness and pain, but there will also be celebration and joy. By seeing the entirety, we actually experience neutrality, which is not the absence of feeling but the sum total of all perspectives.

*Feeling* is the key word here, which isn't what most of us are taught to believe about clarity. For many of us, clarity means seeing things from an "objective" viewpoint, but most such viewpoints are stuck in the human story with a very limited idea of what happened or what's currently happening. What's more, that story is often objective because it's devoid of feeling.

It's not really possible to cut ourselves off from feeling. The person who thinks they're being objective might be caught in an emotional state of cold, buttoned-up rage, or desolation and despair, without even knowing it. What they've really cut themselves off from is the full awareness of all their emotions. And regardless of what people might say, it's not possible to have clarity unless you're clear about what you're feeling and can acknowledge, without judgment, that there might be a different, more high-vibration path to take. This isn't about putting on a smiley face and reaching for the idea of "love and light" (which is what you'll hear a lot of spiritual bypassers talk about, when really, true love and light allow us to connect to all that is, without judgment). It's about giving yourself the space to rage and cry and feel without suppression.

*Emotion* is a word that comes from the Latin *emovere*, which translates to "move out." We are meant to move through and out of our feelings. In fact, an emotion doesn't even stick around that long. It's like an ocean wave that crashes against the shore—powerful at first, but ultimately melting away into sea-foam and wet sand. According to neuroscientist Jill Bolte Taylor, an emotion lasts just 90 seconds; after that, we're making a choice to travel down the same neural pathway, through our thoughts and memories.

The temporary nature of our emotions is deeply healing, even though we don't often see it that way. An emotion is information in motion. It arises to give us insight into what we truly need. To grieve properly, we don't actually need to lie in bed and sulk and stay depressed for six months straight. All we have to do is feel to the core of our being, without suppressing what it is we're feeling. This clears a space for a new experience.

It was a huge revelation for me when I discovered that we don't have to relive our pain over and over until it becomes the new norm. *We just have to feel it.*

Many people who study trauma have suggested that it's just an incomplete survival response that took place when, for whatever reason, the body couldn't do what it needed to do to survive. That's why trauma gets "stuck" in the body—when we're prevented from feeling our feelings all the way through and moving into the natural fight-or-flight response. It might seem like we're holding on to a whole lot of emotion when we're dealing with trauma—and that's part of the problem! We're meant to off-gas those emotions—to literally move them, not get stuck in a constant, repetitive loop! Remember, the ways our past is sabotaging us today are adaptations we created in order to survive. We can choose to elevate and transmute these adaptations so they're no longer a hindrance.

But it's not that simple to learn how to express what we feel, especially if what we feel is big and seemingly uncontainable. But we do ourselves a disservice by holding back. Why do we hold back to begin with? I asked myself this question a lot after my miscarriage, which I mentioned in Chapter 1. There were times when I felt drained and didn't want to feel anything. I came to realize this was partly because I was confused as to why I was feeling such a range of emotions—anger, fear, joy, wonder, and numbness, to name a few. None of it felt like grief! I realized I'd been programmed to believe grief had to look a certain way—so if I felt anything outside that narrow bandwidth, part of me was tempted to clamp down on it.

Instead, I stayed really curious about my experience. I realized that I had unconsciously inherited a very specific idea about what women who'd experienced miscarriages were supposed to feel (i.e., extremely sad, despairing, lost, angry, and so on). *Holy crap,* I thought, *I'm trying to mimic that experience!*

Often, in the attempt to make sense of what we've been through, we contextualize our own experience based on how others have processed similar events. There's nothing wrong with this, but when it takes us away from our own authentic response, or when it causes us to feel that our way of responding isn't the "right" way, we lose clarity and disconnect from our own feelings—which are often far more complex than we think we're allowed to express. When we consider other cultures around the world throughout history, we can see that the experience of grief is much more multifaceted than those in Western culture often allow it to be. The human perception of death is extremely varied, for example—sometimes it's a full-scale celebration of the essence of the human being, which is quite different from mainstream ideas about what it means to be in mourning. When stigma around certain forms of grief gets seeded in a culture, we begin to experience that as our own reality. This could be labeled as the collective consciousness or simply social learning, which can be inauthentic at times, even in something as precious as loss.

We need to be really clear about the story our feelings are telling. And often, that story is a big one with lots of moving parts. And it's a smaller story that sits inside the loving palm of the divine story. We ourselves sit in a much more grand and vast reality than we acknowledge. There's always another reality available to us, even when we forget it exists. We can choose whether we become the frequency of this limited reality, or whether we exercise curiosity to get to clarity about the grander scope of things.

There's a range of experiences available to us, but our consciousness tends to default to a pretty narrow bandwidth based on conscious and unconscious ideas we absorbed about what it is acceptable to feel. Even if we can't change the particularities of any experience, we can always change our perception of what's happening.

If someone says to me, "Well, Mandy, all I can see and feel is pain," I can completely accept that. Their feelings are absolutely valid. However, we always have a choice. We can remain in this singular perception, or we can start to expand incrementally to the point at which more possibilities are accessible to us—the same way Maria did when she began to move out of the tunnel vision of her grief. Perhaps we'll even be able to see the beauty and joy that are available in the midst of the pain. Many of us are resistant to feeling that beauty and joy because we think we need to be loyal to our pain for it to be genuine. But this is a mistaken belief. The divine light allows us to have many different responses to the same experience and see our journey as an unfolding process of discovery, where we get to connect to higher and higher states of consciousness through our willingness to be with all of it.

## Reflection Questions

1. How aware are you of your full range of emotions during any given experience? Do you usually focus on the "strongest" one, or do you pay attention to everything that might be happening?

2. Can you think of any times you've defaulted to a particular emotional state because of any social messaging you absorbed around the feelings that were appropriate to that experience?

3. How might this idea about the "right" way to feel have clashed with the full scope of what you were actually feeling?

## GET CLEAR AND EXPRESS YOURSELF

If there's one thing I want to emphasize about this pathway, it's that one of the quickest paths to clarity is also one of the least intuitive—the path of our emotions. A lot of us have been conditioned to think that emotion is incompatible with clarity. We think of clarity as being objective rather than a perception that arises from our open hearts. But the more we open up to our emotions, the more of our emotions we'll have access to. This is what will allow us to sit with the complexity of the big picture and wrap our heads and hearts and spirits around all of it.

If we've been taught to clamp down on our emotions, opening up to and expressing them might be challenging. But that's why we have amazing channels like art. When we read a poem, watch a movie, or listen to a song, a world of emotions is evoked. We do have to be careful about not getting stuck in those emotions, like when we listen to an ex's favorite album on repeat after a difficult breakup. Thankfully, art is time bound. The subconscious mind knows the song ends in five minutes or the movie is over in two hours. This gives us an opportunity to walk through the storm of our emotions and to let ourselves be there. Art accompanies us in the process of expressing what's been on lockdown.

How do you know when you've fully expressed something that has been needing to move all the way through but has never had the opportunity? You feel the peace and release that's possible after a really good cry. You'll feel more settled, and you'll no longer be in the clutches of an oppressive emotion. Peace is an equilibrium point between a number of different emotional states; it's like balancing in the center of the seesaw. That's why peace is such an important component of clarity.

There may be times when we find that we need to do a whole lot of expressing until we move out of the pressure-cooker sensation of being caught in a single difficult emotion. But the pressure will alleviate the more we allow the emotion to simply move through our system—because as we express it, we are meeting its need to be seen, which means it will stop clouding our vision and capacity to see more clearly. It always comes back to the intention we set for ourselves.

You don't need to know where your emotions are coming from or even if they've been around for a long time. All you have to do is ask yourself if the emotion still feels authentic to you, or if it equates to a good life. Is staying stuck in this emotion bringing you closer to the light or taking you further from it? It's necessary to recognize whether we're being self-destructive by losing ourselves inside the false comfort of a dominant emotion, thus reopening a wound instead of healing it, and when we're genuinely allowing it to shift and dissipate. We'll get better and better at determining this the more we attune to our bodies and register whether there's an actual release. It isn't the action we take that matters, but rather the energy behind it that will determine our experience.

Often, when we're reopening a wound, we are counter-intuitively doing something to numb our experience of the feeling. Someone who feels stuck in self-hatred might decide to "express" it by taking drugs or drinking themselves into a stupor. This does nothing to move the emotion of self-hatred; in fact, it momentarily numbs the person to the experience of self-hatred but doesn't actually change or alleviate the feeling state. It's important to understand that sometimes the intention to move through an emotion will first intensify the associated sensations, because we're no longer trying to numb our awareness. Instead of turning to the bottle, an alcoholic who's experiencing withdrawal symptoms might choose to redirect their energy toward something like vigorous exercise or unburdening their thoughts to a support group.

In the wake of my dad's death, I chose to express agony in real time rather than making the mistake of putting it on ice. My 12-year-old son sometimes remarks, "Remember when you'd go outside and scream at the top of your lungs?" I was that raw and real with myself. My dad loved Johnny Cash, so I'd listen to his music and bawl my eyes out whenever I felt I needed to. There was momentum to my grieving. I chose to move the energy with as much passion and spontaneity as I could muster. I walked on the bare earth, wrote my dad letters, vigorously shook and cried and screamed . . . and in just two weeks, the rawness was gone. It was replaced by clarity and acceptance. Now that I had finally grieved my dad, I was ready to integrate the bigger picture of the gift that he had been to me. I could see that inside my grief were the seeds of the divine light that was living inside me through my loving memory of him.

## PRACTICE: GET CLEAR AND EXPRESS YOURSELF

1. Think of a situation in your life where you felt caught in an overwhelming and burdensome emotion. This might be guilt, grief, shame, fear, or even desire. Take some time to write about this experience, and how it might be keeping you from the divine balm of clarity.

2. Write out a list of all the ways you're going to choose to let your emotion move through you and fully express itself. Separate the list into different categories: spiritual (prayer, conversations with the divine, meditation, breathwork, etc.), mental/emotional (journaling, reading poetry, listening to music, making art, watching a film that helps you to move that stagnant energy, talking to a trusted friend or counselor, etc.), physical (dancing, making love, being outside in nature, sleeping, screaming at the top of your lungs, etc.).

3. If what you're feeling is a difficult or sharp emotion and you don't know how to express it in a healthy way that keeps you from acting out against yourself or others, don't despair. Honor the emotion by saying to yourself, "There's a reason for what I'm feeling, and it's valid from a human perspective, but I'm going to take this particular action—and my intention behind the action is to release or better understand and process the energy of my emotion so it no longer lives inside me."

4. Now, give yourself at least a week to engage in your chosen activities, setting the intention to fully express what has been locked inside you.

5. Be deeply honest with yourself as you observe what is happening. Are you feeling a sense of release? Or are you getting locked inside the emotion? If the latter is the case, continue to set the intention to move the emotion all the way

through. Be sure to ask yourself if the actions you're taking are aligned with an energy of divine release rather than self-sabotage.

6. At the end of the week (or the time period you've allotted to fully expressing yourself), take note of how you feel. Are you at peace? Is there a greater sense of clarity? A broader awareness of the full spectrum of your emotions? Remember that learning to move through the cycle of a dominant emotion can take time and practice. Be patient with yourself and continue to do what needs to be done.

## YOUR DIVINE LIGHT PRACTICE

Repeat the *Get Clear and Express Yourself* practice. You can work with one or several dominant emotions that feel stuck inside you, but work with only one at a time. Be patient and gentle with this practice, especially if you have difficulty opening up and letting your feelings come to the surface. Consider seeking the help of a supportive counselor or wise guide who can help you deal with whatever you're feeling.

As always, take time to revisit the reflection questions at the end of each section in this chapter, and to journal on them.

## Takeaways

1.  The fourth pathway of light, **clarity**, represents
    the vast panorama of everything that exists.
    It helps us attune to the full spectrum of our
    emotions and to hold the complexity of our
    experience with awe and wonder.

2.  The highest form of clarity is the frequency of
    truth—and even when it feels like it's difficult
    to face the truth, or that the truth will hurt
    people in your life, choosing it will always be in
    the greatest good of all involved. It is only our
    fear-based decisions that lead to pain.

3.  Even when we're stuck inside a painful
    experience that feels like it will never end, it's
    always our choice as to whether or not we'll
    stay stuck. When we begin to dive into the
    reasons we're stuck and to question the solidity
    of our narrative, we start to gain clarity and free
    ourselves from the trap of thinking our pain
    will last forever.

4.  One of the greatest ways to determine whether
    we're making the right decision for ourselves is
    to sense if it feels heavy or light. The lighter our
    decisions, the clearer and brighter we can shine
    our light.

5.  One of the fastest ways to get to clarity is by
    making ourselves available to the full range of
    our emotions and accepting the complexity
    of our experience—remembering that the

divine light encompasses sadness and pain,
but also celebration and joy. When we come to
understand this, we experience neutrality and
peace, which is the sum total of all perspectives.

6.   When we allow ourselves to fully express the
     emotions locked up within us, we discover that
     we can cycle through difficult or burdensome
     feelings with greater ease and rapidity, as we
     were always meant to. When we do this, we
     come to a place of equilibrium that allows us to
     be in contact with all of our feelings.

# CHAPTER 5

# transmutation

Even if you're surrounded by darkness, just take the next illuminated step. No matter what we've done or how much darkness lives in our past, that past does not and cannot ultimately define us. We have the capacity to transmute some of our most painful experiences into our most meaningful gifts. After all, darkness is just light that has forgotten itself. Every experience is an opportunity for illumination, and it doesn't require making a journey to the other side of the world if it feels like night where you are. The light is never far away, as it resides within our very being.

The divine light within us will never work to negate our human story, no matter how dark and bereft it may feel. We know there is very real suffering in our lives and on the planet, and it's not useful to spiritually bypass our way through our stumbling blocks. Instead, the divine gives us a beautiful container in which to place our human story—a container that helps us grow and that connects us with even more of who we *really* are and what we can choose to be.

This is the power of the light; it isn't there just for the people who are happy and living in their purpose at all times. In truth, the light lives in every desolate place, and sometimes that's where it shines the brightest. If you're stumbling through a cold and lonely maze inside your inner world and turn over any rock that's there, you'll find the gem of your divine truth, waiting for you to grab hold of it and share its beauty with others. Our gifts are always present, even when we ourselves do not want to be.

When we transmute the sticky parts of our human story, we release our unhealed parts from suffering; we come home to ourselves. The light within is an ally in our unfolding process, and **transmutation** (the process of changing from a low-vibration state to a high-vibration one, usually by transforming the meaning we've attached to our experience) is a pathway that helps us to feel the strength and warmth of that light. Every time we're willing to transmute our pain for the purpose of connecting with the divine and being our authentic selves on this planet, we magnify the light within us so that it becomes a beacon for all living beings.

How do we commit to being that kind of brilliant way-shower who lights the lantern so others can locate the ground and find their way home? Too often, we think we need to be the smartest or wisest or most charismatic person in the room in order to help others, but this couldn't be further from the truth. I realized I could help other people when I began to share my rawest and most painful memories. I learned that when we make meaning from our suffering, and when we turn our despair into hope and beauty, it becomes our greatest service to the world.

It's our way of assuring others who are hurting that they aren't broken; that they are, in fact, tender and precious and worthy, and they have everything they need to get through this moment.

I learned this lesson in an unexpected way when I reconnected with my dad as an adult. When I was young, I always viewed my dad as my hero. He was smart, handsome, rugged, and so strong. I was the dutiful daughter, and in my eyes, he could do no wrong. Little did I realize that my dad had struggled with addiction my entire life. I was unwilling to view him through anything less than rose-tinted glasses, especially because I was so angry and resentful toward my mom, whom I'd cast in the role of villain. But over the course of my life, his superhero mask began to slip and my ideas about my dad fell apart.

When I was 13, Dad called to tell me he'd overdosed on a bottle of Percocet. I didn't know how to take this, especially because he didn't explain why it had happened. I simply internalized it to mean that there must be something wrong with me if my super strong, awesome father didn't want to live any longer. I didn't see him as anything less than the man I'd always loved and admired. I just blamed myself for not being good enough for him to want to live for.

While the facade crumbled even more as I grew older and realized that I'd had only a sliver of the bigger picture of his relationship with Mom, I still continued to feel nothing but love for him. However, the distance between us had grown, while the distance between me and Mom had narrowed because of all the internal and external work we'd done to align with the light and each other. Dad had been through seven marriages, and he'd cheated on and financially taken advantage of all his wives. He was constantly living hand to mouth, and he had numerous debts that remained unpaid. Dad was a complicated man, but I still loved him. I was able to hold the complexity of him in my heart. On the one hand, he was an interesting and adventurous man who'd seemingly lived many lives wrapped into one, but a part of his free-spirited nature and wildness had come from hurting so many people, especially the women in his life.

When Oliver and I got married, I didn't hesitate to invite Dad to the wedding. I hadn't seen him in at least six years, and I knew he was in poor health. In contrast, I was better than I'd ever been: financially, emotionally, spiritually. After the wedding, Dad reached out to thank me for the invitation. I responded that it had meant so much to me that he'd come, as I'd feared that I wouldn't be able to dance with him on my wedding day.

Then, the conversation took a strange turn. "You know, I was talking to your uncle, and I told him that you drive an Aston Martin. That's an expensive car!" he remarked.

"Yeah, I guess so," I said, not knowing where the conversation was headed.

"Plus, you guys have a multimillion-dollar home!"

It was starting to feel pretty awkward.

"I'm so glad you're doing so well, because I've always wanted the best for my little girl," he went on. "My truck recently broke down, but knowing you're set makes me happy."

I immediately replied, "Dad, I know you spent money flying to the wedding. Why don't I pay for your truck to get fixed?"

He was grateful for the offer and took me up on it, but during that conversation, something in our dynamic changed. I could feel the energy shift, and it was uncomfortable . . . but I didn't want to face what was happening. He was my father, and I just wanted to be there for him. I sent him money to repair his truck. A few weeks passed before he asked for a few thousand more dollars for some other reason. It kept happening every couple weeks without fail. He had a new excuse each time. Because I wanted to be a good daughter and I'd been conditioned to believe that kids should care for their parents to a certain extent, I acquiesced. But over time, I had the sense that what I was doing was . . . wrong, somehow.

I had worked with clients who shared similar issues about their relationship with their parents, so I started to consider what I might say to such a person. I certainly wouldn't suggest that they unfailingly keep bailing that parent out; having the money to do so wasn't really the point, either. The energetic pattern that gets set up when this kind of one-sided expectation continues to be met is highly dysfunctional. I told Dad that I'd buy him groceries and do whatever I could to help him take care of his necessities, but I was no longer going to send him cash. He hadn't paid me back for any of what he'd "borrowed," and I had no idea where any of the money was really going or if it was being used to perpetuate his addictions. Dad accused me of psychoanalyzing him. I could tell there was something wrong—he would slur his words during our phone calls and then revert back to his normal self. As he persisted in his attempts to convince me, I could feel something I hadn't felt before: the version of Dad that every woman who'd been involved with him had likely encountered.

A voice inside me said, "Mandy, you need to step out of the human perception of being his daughter. Go to your soul, which is pure light, and imagine yourself face-to-face with his soul, which is also pure light. From that place, ask yourself what needs to happen in this dynamic."

One of my gifts is to help people break the chains their soul gets stuck in so they can find their own way back to the light. Dad had a lifelong pattern of using women financially. I could tell that he was at the end of his life, and I couldn't be another woman who refused to stand up to him or didn't try to break this vicious cycle by speaking my truth. So, I decided then and there to step into my gift and to transmute the relationship I'd had with him—a relationship that had not entirely been based on authenticity.

"Dad, this is a soulful lesson you need to learn before you die. You hurt women and use them for their money." As I said these words, I could tell that they cut him to his very core. Just as I'd seen Dad as the apple of my eye, I had long suspected that I was his favorite child—but his feelings were based on the fact that I had never challenged him. I knew that it hurt him to see that his doting daughter didn't respect him in the way he thought a father should be respected. However, as kind as I tried to be, I didn't temper my honesty. My soul knew that my words were cracking open a potential for healing, as painful as that moment was. Just as I felt I was transmuting our relationship from a place of love, I knew I had to give Dad's soul the opportunity to step up and transmute the toxicity of his pattern.

Dad didn't react well. He said, "Mandy, for crying out loud, I'm only asking for a hundred bucks! If I don't get it to these people I owe money to, I'll be in big trouble. Don't you realize they're after me?"

I felt sad that he still couldn't be honest with me, but I held my ground. I breathed a huge sigh of relief when I hung up. I'd just done one of the hardest things I'd ever done. Oliver held me and smiled with the utmost pride and sympathy. Dad was at a low point, but my soul understood that giving in and giving him what he wanted was not the same as helping him. Even if he didn't recognize the gift, I did. I wasn't playing the role he'd cast me in. I was standing in my light, and I was inviting him to stand in his. If I continued to succumb to his pattern, the human part of him would reap the rewards while ensuring that he'd take that pattern with him to the grave. There was no way I was going to be a participant in that kind of karma.

Remarkably, even though we didn't speak to each other after that, I unexpectedly received a check from him for $100 shortly after that call. A month passed, and I received another check in the same amount. I didn't cash either check (after all, Dad was barely getting by on his Social Security benefits), but I knew when I received them that this was his way of demonstrating his soul had learned the lesson. He was choosing love over money, perhaps for the first time in his life. I called him to say that he didn't need to pay me back, but I just needed to know I was more important to him than the money. "It means so much to me," I said, "and I know you might not see this, but it means a lot for *you* that you chose to do this." The conversation was short, but some part of me felt that he received the message, loud and clear. We said we loved each other, and that was the last I ever heard from Dad. He died six weeks later.

Of course, there's a human part of me that wishes we'd had the opportunity to develop a brand-new relationship and that he'd gotten a chance to turn his life around in dramatic ways. But what matters most to me is the feeling and experience of love that permeated my heart during our final conversation. I'm sure he felt it, too, even if he didn't have the clarity to talk about it. I could feel that something had been lifted off of me—a weight I hadn't realized I'd been carrying. I transmuted my relationship with Dad by refusing to stumble around in the darkness of patterns that were based in fear and avoidance. I turned to my soul to find the light, which changed everything.

## GIFT SHIFT THEORY

I believe the reason I was able to transmute my relationship with my dad and bring it to a more honest and soul-centered place is due to something I call *gift shift theory*. The term refers to the idea that a quality or aspect of our history that may once have wounded us can become our greatest gift.

Perhaps a person experienced intense trauma in their early life, and their shame has caused them to push the experience away, or to pull toward themselves a "better" life. This push-and-pull approach can keep us in a state of resistance, as it's rooted in a lack of acceptance of what happened to us. When we find the light, we start to see that traumatized part of ourselves as something that has forgotten its true nature as light. In this way, the person who has lived with complex trauma can learn to step into their light, without shame or blame, and the very thing they once encountered as dense and debilitating can be transmuted. They can now use that painful experience as a way to help others who are similarly hurting. They can see that while they suffered in the past, it's possible to view their story from multiple angles (for example, their pain helped them develop greater compassion for both victims and perpetrators, who each suffer in unique ways). This is how we come to transmute the coal of our suffering into our greatest treasure: a sense of purpose that can become our service to the world. Transmutation helps us elevate our feelings of worthlessness and loneliness so they can become the launchpad for our genius. In the words of someone I once heard, "I'm sorry God has so much faith in you."

This was what happened to me. The moment I decided to move out of "Mandy as daughter" and into "Mandy as soul," I saw that I had a divine gift that helped me to mirror the light to other people so they could find their way back to their true selves. I wasn't able to do this because I'd lived some kind of charmed life where nothing ever hurt. Quite the opposite! I'd stumbled around in my own personal maze of darkness for years, and it hurt like heck! But in the midst of the hurt, I discovered an unbelievable expansiveness that I would come to recognize as the divine. I found that even at my lowest low, there was a beautiful light that would always remind me of my innate perfection and wholeness. I didn't have to be perfect or, to paraphrase the wonderful poet Mary Oliver, get on my hands and knees and walk through the desert in repentance to prove my "goodness." I wanted other people who felt similarly broken to realize the same was true for them—that this transformation could happen in an instant instead of through years of self-imposed punishment or attempts to try to be a better person. The divine will welcome us home whenever we're ready to come back—and I wanted to be the kind of person who gave people a road map to home.

The divine has given us so many gifts . . . and there are infinite ways to unlock them. Some of the most potent gifts we have are only unlocked in our darkest moments, which, to me, is a beautiful metaphor for the divine itself.

The light is always there—it's just up to us to acknowledge it. Gift shift theory is one of the ways we can do this. That doesn't mean it negates our suffering at all—but it does give us a way to move through it so we can help others who are in pain. One of the greatest ways we can help people is to transmute our own trauma into a gift that empowers and lifts them up. This is how we also transmute the larger human story of density and separation from the divine and bring it back to the light of pure, awakened consciousness.

There were times when all I could see were the rough patches of my human story, which was riddled with density and disappointment. It was really easy to get lost in the ways my life had messed me up. The mess ups were all I could see. But then, I came to realize that the entirety of my worldview had been skewed. The light of my personal sun had been blotted out by the darkness of my victimhood story—my belief that life never worked out for me. But disempowerment is the opposite of catalyzing our gifts and using them for the betterment of all. I realized that I wanted to be the kind of person who could intentionally utilize and direct my consciousness to that which I desired, not that which I didn't.

Interestingly, people who are miserable tend to step into the world of Manifestation 101 to get away from the experience of their trauma. Their brain is neurologically wired to create an energy field that consistently pumps out thoughts and beliefs attached to the story of their trauma. Sometimes, people who work with the Law of Attraction and other principles of manifestation are able to move through their trauma and step into their gifts—but other times, they're working with a pattern of resistance that accomplishes the opposite of what they want. As the saying goes, what we resist persists!

Collectively, we're beginning to evolve into a new space of understanding. Instead of separating from the thing that caused us pain, we're learning to integrate a new understanding of life. I see this with my clients and students all the time. They start to make peace with the part of their story from which they'd dissociated (the part that used to make them go, "That was wrong. That was painful. I don't even want to think about it!") or that they're still overly fixating on (with sentiments like, "That totally sucked! Why does bad stuff always happen to me? I'm so angry at my parents, God—or whatever—for doing this to me!"). Instead, they start to see that this aspect they'd negated or cursed is a vital piece of their entire intricate story—it's not the entirety of who they are, but it's a beautiful thread in it. They also begin to realize that they can tell their story in a brand-new way. They can say, "I might not have had a choice back then, but here's what I'm going to do with it now."

Krysta was part of a group attunement (energy work) that I did with a large number of people. Krysta had a history of sexual abuse. During an attunement, I ask clients to see the tapestry of their life laid out in front of them. When she did this, the abuse she'd experienced sat front and center, taking up most of the scene. She continued to pour love over the tapestry and to experience the presence of divine energy as she listened to my words. As she later told me, her tapestry did something it had never done before. It began to change. The ugly, decrepit image of her abuse transformed. Now, it was positively glowing. There were bright, crisp colors, and flowers had been planted to replace the previously dismal and lifeless scene. Everything looked fresh and new. The image of her abuse had shrunk and moved to a corner of her tapestry so that it was no longer front and center. She allowed her human story to stay, but to be transmuted so that it was no longer the entire story. When Krysta shared this with the group, I could see that her entire demeanor had also transformed. I could see her wholeness and beauty shining through. In sitting with the painful story and allowing the light to gradually come in and transform her tapestry, Krysta had accessed the gift in the midst of the pain: an abiding, unconditional sense of divine love and wonder.

Again, none of this detracts from the fact that Krysta or any of us have suffered along our journey. Maybe we went through hell to get to where we are today. And if we were victimized, this doesn't excuse the people or forces that contributed to the harm we experienced. Yes, that reality gets to stay, but now it's sitting inside the broader and infinitely larger field of light. And that's part of the gift, too! There's a home for our sadness and disappointment. There's a built-in comfort that we get to experience when we embrace the bigger picture of the truth. Now, the story we hold isn't just about our victimization. It's also about our resilience, strength, and capacity to help others who might be in the same shoes we used to be in. From this place, we—and nobody else—get to define our own gifts. It's like taking a sponge and wringing out so much more from it than what we thought was originally present. Our original perception doesn't have to completely disappear for this to happen; it simply has to come into contact with the light of the divine.

## Reflection Questions

1. What is one of the greatest pains or traumas you've lived through? How has it impacted your life? (Don't feel you need to dig into every detail, and only go there if you feel safe to do so.)

2. Knowing that you absolutely have the right to acknowledge the depth of your suffering, can you expand your perspective so you can also see the gifts you uncovered in the midst of this dark experience? What was the light that was present for you all along? Name it and claim it for yourself.

3. How can you use this gift to serve others who might be going through the same thing, or something similar? How do you want to use this gift? (It may help to get outside and put your bare feet on the ground as you ponder this, or after you've done a nice guided meditation.)

4. How does this shift make you feel—physically, mentally, emotionally, and spiritually?

## WHAT'S YOUR CURRENCY?

One of the major things that keeps us from fully catalyzing our gifts and standing in our light is a sense of guilt. We continue to pay for our perceived wrongs in the past—just like I did after my abortion.

I often ask students or clients: "What's your currency?" This is how I define the energy they're using to pay for what they did in the past. Often, it's not a high-vibration energy and tends to come in the form of an emotional violence we wield against ourselves or others.

Caroline was a middle-aged woman who was grappling with the fact that her daughter, Sabrina, had been molested by her own father as a young child. Caroline blamed herself for not protecting her daughter from her husband, whose abuse she only learned about years later. Caroline wondered if she had been willfully blind or ignorant. Every day, she made a litany of all the ways she'd failed Sabrina. I was astonished as I heard Caroline beating herself up. She seemed to be forgetting that Sabrina was now a grown woman who had a successful and meaningful career as a therapist who bravely and gently walked other people through their trauma. When I tried to remind Caroline about this, she reverted to the same excuses. "I'll never live a beautiful life after what I did to my daughter . . . after what I allowed him to do to her," she insisted.

I tried to help Caroline see that her currency was guilt, which was a very low-vibration currency. She seemed to believe that it was a zero-sum game. That is, in order for Sabrina to heal or experience some kind of justice, Caroline herself needed to remain unhealed and broken. I explained that she could go the route of forever attempting to pay for her "sin" with this seemingly endless stream of guilt (which never felt like enough), or she could change her currency altogether. "What if your currency was helping other people? What if you rectified that wrong in a way that was actually of benefit to the most people possible?" I asked.

Caroline had been stuck in the darkness for so long, but now, she had a lifeline. She could see that the light was in reach. Her heart was full of love, and she wanted to be able to share it with others, including her daughter, in a way that actually served them. She was also creating a burden for Sabrina, who felt she had to constantly seem happy and healed so her mother didn't spiral into more shame; this ultimately kept Sabrina stuck in a different way. Caroline realized that her story of not being deserving of redemption—of having to pay for her mistakes with her very life energy—had blocked her from what was possible: the ability to truly be an exemplar of love and healing on this planet. Over time, Caroline became a very talented practitioner through one of my certification programs, and she was able to heal her relationship with Sabrina. But before she could do this, she had to step into the space of acknowledging that she was not everything she had ever done (back to Chapter 2 and the power of self-knowledge!). She had a responsibility to contribute to the collective in a positive manner rather than the way she'd been trying to account for her so-called mistakes, which ensured she'd never get to her desired destination.

As I taught Caroline, your currency is literally the energy you are putting into the world. We have all done things we felt we needed to pay for, and this isn't a bad thing. After all, our currency could be all about spreading joy, comfort, kindness, and care. The light within us will never ask us to sacrifice our own happiness and well-being to pay for our errors; in fact, it is only when we step into the light—where abundance, grace, and connection are ever present—that we can truly share our gifts with the world! We have to transmute our own misplaced, albeit well-meaning, ideas about how we can best serve the world if we ever want to be a positive force on this planet.

This is not about "evening the playing field" by choosing self-punishment. Remember the saying, "An eye for an eye makes the whole world blind"? When we attempt to right an imbalance by harming ourselves, we only end up perpetuating low-vibration energy. We're trying to make up for the past by identifying with an incorrect version of self. But to make sense of the world, the human mind tends to think in terms of constructs and comparisons. This all goes back to what we discussed in Chapter 2—that is, we wrongly interpret the past through the lens of "There's something wrong with me," or "I did something bad," which is a supremely egotistical way to go about looking at the world.

When I was much younger and worked as a personal trainer, I worked with another young woman who was financially supported by a man who was extremely generous with his money. I went out with them and a group of other people, and he gave me $1,000 worth of Visa gift cards without so much as blinking. I thought it was odd and turned to my client to ask her what was going on, as this went above and beyond paying for everyone else's meal. "Don't worry, he does this with everyone—it's just how he is," she told me.

He was very forthright when I thanked him. He said, "I've done a lot of bad things in my life, and I'm just trying to even the score."

Now, I have no idea what kind of things he'd done, but I was glad that his self-awareness had become fuel for generosity instead of more heinous behavior. That money helped me buy a kitchen table and a computer for school, and it meant more than he probably knew. In his own way, he was transmuting darkness by being a force for good who expected nothing in return and simply wanted to balance the scales to the best of his ability. For even when we've done "bad" things, there's always so much more to us than the past. There's purity and goodness that resides within us; this is our light to share with the world, and it's our responsibility to do so in the best way we can.

## Reflection Questions

1. Is there anything in your past that you regret doing (or not doing)? With the utmost compassion, think about the currency you're using to pay for this experience.

2. What is the effect of that currency on yourself and others? Does it have a contracting or an expanding energy? Is it of a low or high vibration? What kind of impact does it have on you and others?

3. Consider that it might be time to pay for the past with a brand-new currency. What kind of currency do you want to put out into the world, so that you can be of service and ensure that you and others get to reap the benefits of your light?

## MAKING THE SHIFT TO STAND IN THE LIGHT

Just as I experienced with my dad, something truly magical happens when we make the shift to stand inside our soul, where we access the light of the divine. This may well be the greatest transmutation we can encounter, and it's pretty magical—it's like transforming on the same level as what happens to Cinderella. (Side note: I've always believed that story is a metaphor for what happens when we stand in the light of our authentic self, no matter what the circumstances of our life might be. Although Cinderella's family hurts her and treats her as "less than," her fairy godmother gives her the magical tools to step fully into her authentic self, her soul—which is what the prince sees when he falls in love with her.) At the same time, it can be challenging—especially if we've made unconscious contracts with ourselves and others to behave in disempowering ways, usually for the purpose of ensuring connection, love, or a sense of belonging. But relationships based on inauthenticity are never for anyone's highest good because they keep us stuck in a very limited version of ourselves.

Since I shifted into utilizing my gifts, I haven't been afraid to use "tough love" if I know it's for the other person's greatest or highest good—even if there's the possibility that they will resent me or cut off the relationship. When I know that my actions are for their highest good, I do it, because this is my way of upholding my end of our soul contract and reminding them of their light. (More about that in Chapter 7, where I discuss how the frequency of truth, aka the highest good, attunes us to the frequency of love and coherence!)

How do you know you're standing in your soul and doing something for the highest good? Well, it's never a logical or intellectual decision. It's an embodied knowing that requires courage. Once you do this, even if it's very hard, you'll experience a feeling of lightness rather than the heaviness associated with being inauthentic. The magic of standing inside the truth of your soul is that it allows you to step into your full power and potential. When you live from the light of your soul, you no longer need to pretend to be someone you're not—or to stand by and perpetuate a toxic pattern. Because the light of truth and love are on your side, you can show up fully and authentically, without fear of judgment or rejection. This kind of freedom is truly liberating, not just for you but also for other people.

When I was interacting with my dad, there was something about this deep soul knowing that radiated through my entire being, when I finally confronted my dad even though I didn't want to hurt his feelings. Once you see a pattern, you can't just unsee it. I realized that I wasn't doing what a loving daughter would do. Playing "nice" and accommodating him was not helping him; in fact, it was contributing to his misery because it perpetuated his feelings of separation—which were locked inside his tendency to lie, cheat, and swindle his way through life at the expense of his relationships. This pattern had caused him so much pain, and I refused to contribute to it anymore. Standing in my light meant that I was willing to see Dad's light too. While I was willing to help him, I wasn't going to keep giving him an excuse to stay stuck in his addictive patterns.

I see this same pattern at work among parents of children with addiction issues. They often want to "fix" their children's problems, but when I help them to redirect their attention to healing themselves instead, just about every single one has the experience of their kids getting clean. The hardest lesson that many parents have to learn is that their children are unique souls on their own individual journeys. The greatest gift a parent can give their child is their commitment to their own personal healing. Addictive patterns are often unconsciously tied to trauma within the family of origin—and when a parent does their work to find their way back to the light, it has ripple effects.

Irene once came to me seeking help for her son Sam, who was addicted to heroin. I gently told her, "I know you want to help Sam, but you're actually contributing to his addiction by trying to save him and bail him out. Let's focus on you instead. Heal whatever patterns are in you that might be contributing to Sam's addiction. Because when you try to save him, you see how he moves further away from you. That cat-and-mouse pattern is actually contributing to the addiction."

Irene committed to going through my certification program, and to helping other families who were trying to heal patterns of addiction—but it took moving her attention away from saving Sam to dealing with her own unresolved childhood trauma. Today, Sam is gradually getting better and learning to heal and step into his own power—just as Irene is intentionally engaging in her own growth journey. Irene recently told me, "I realize the connection between parent and child is so primal and complicated, because sometimes you don't know where you end and they begin. But I really began to see the ways I was accidentally contributing to his addiction. I realized I was stuck in some of my own unhelpful patterns. The more I released these patterns, the more I saw how I was granting him the ability to see new possibilities."

Standing in our soul requires doing exactly what Irene did: we need to see what the unhelpful pattern we're partaking in is. Then, with an attitude of surrender, we can take a few steps back and recognize that there's a different way that opens us up to greater ease and possibility. This is true for all the souls who might be involved.

Too often, we're in relationship with a false projection of another person. The unhealed part of us dances with the unhealed part of them because we made the unconscious agreement that this was the only way we could connect. True connection only comes from standing in our soul and transmuting the toxic ties that masqueraded as love. The soul sees with clarity and candor that this will not do—there is a better way.

It's an amazing experience when your desire to stand in the light of your soul is greater than your desire to "keep the peace" (which was never peace to begin with). But it does require doing something to break the toxic pattern. Sometimes, that means stepping away from an existing relationship and making space for a new pattern to be created. There will be occasions when the other person in question has no desire to make the necessary changes for a new, healthy relationship, but I promise that on the level of the soul, you've done more good than you can see—even if you never get the opportunity to experience those benefits firsthand. You had a soul-to-soul connection, and this cannot help but open the door a little wider so that when the other person is ready, they can follow the light home.

## Reflection Questions

1.  Think of a difficult relationship or situation you might be facing. What are the patterns at play?

2.  Imagine your soul/higher self standing face-to-face with the other person's soul/higher self. See and feel this as if it's happening in real time. What does your soul wish to communicate?

3.  What might be holding you back from standing in your soul with this person or situation?

4.  What might be the benefits of choosing authenticity over convenience and making the shift to stand in your soul?

The magic of standing inside the truth of your soul is that it allows you to step into your full power and potential.

## ACCESS YOUR GIFTS AND PURPOSE

One of the great gifts of transmuting the darkness of our experiences into the light of our expanded awareness is that we feel connected to a deeper sense of purpose. There's something much bigger than fear or regret that drives our actions and way of being in the world.

Unfortunately, people get stuck on the idea that they need to know their purpose and be accurate about whatever they choose (as if life were a one-time deal and we only have one shot to get it right!). People ask me about their purpose all the time, to which I jokingly respond, "I'm not a crystal ball!"

Trust me, I get the need to know. One of my greatest fears before I started serving in the way I do today was that I'd leave the planet not having done what I came here for: to serve the greatest number of people possible by helping them find the light within. Lots of people have the same fear. The thing I had to remember is this: our purpose is divine! We can't use it as a way to satisfy the egoic human need to feel certain that we're living our purpose.

The truth is, our soul always knows our purpose. If we are unclear, this is usually because some part of us is avoiding the sense of responsibility that might come from living in our purpose . . . as well as the changes that doing so would bring about.

Sometimes, I'll ask someone, "Even if I told you that I could see your purpose,"—which sometimes happens, although I never feel it's my place to tell anyone what they should be doing—"would you actually listen to me and live your life in a way that's aligned with that purpose?"

Often, they look at me like I'm crazy. "What are you talking about? Of course, I would!"

Then, I might say, with a totally straight face, "Quit your job. And leave your toxic marriage."

That's when they hesitate.

So often, it's not that we don't know our purpose or that we haven't been accessing our gifts in some way. It's that we've constructed falsehoods to ensure that we won't get to the place where we want to be. Sometimes that sounds like, "I'll have to change everything in my life if I want to live in my purpose, and that'll be too hard." But, when you're living in the light, the things you used to believe would be difficult become super easy. I used to fear rejection and vulnerability, but when I stepped into my next level of growth, I realized that I couldn't care less about dealing with haters on the Internet. Everything I feared seemed petty in retrospect, compared to the importance of serving someone in the depths of their pain or growth.

Many of us have a lot of false ideas about what it would take to live our purpose and what we might need to sacrifice, all because we're living in our human story. Years ago, I wrote out a business plan centered around the therapy clinics I wanted to open, using a template that asked me a series of questions. I came to the question, "What's the main thing holding you back?" My response was: "Time, time, time!" I was working 16-hour days, and I just didn't have the time to implement my plan. I perceived that I probably needed to clear my calendar altogether to fulfill such a huge ambition. In retrospect, I realize that time was a logical excuse not to move forward with my idea, so that I wouldn't have to risk rejection or failure. (Although, I realize that today, I'm doing exactly what I said I wanted to do through my coaching certification program, even if the format is very different from what I'd initially imagined!)

Stepping into purpose requires another transmutation: shifting from the head and into the heart. Most people who say, "I want to know my purpose," are still living in their human story of how it should look and what it might take to get there. So, instead of focusing on the details, I ask, "What is it you want the world to feel?" I know that for myself, I want the world to feel loved; I want people to feel they are enough, just as they are. (No surprise that this is how I also wanted to feel when I was at my lowest!)

Then, they might say, "I want other people to appreciate what it's like to step into someone else's shoes, even if that person is really different from them. I want the world to feel tolerance, love, and respect for diversity."

I'll respond, "Okay, now we're getting somewhere. Consider it your job to go out and be that frequency. Be that embodiment of tolerance, love, and respect, and not just when other people are looking or when you have an audience. If you want others to feel that way, give it to them."

Of course, this person might realize they need to write a book about tolerance and respect to live out their purpose—and this might be true, but we can often get stymied by a big vision when our human story crops up and gets in the way. This is why I suggest that people go back to the basics and focus on how to bring forth the feeling they connect with their purpose. We do this, first and foremost, by embodying the qualities we want to teach or nurture in others.

When we decide what we want the world to feel, we become our purpose. From my experience, it's when we do this the platforms where we can express our purpose in the 3D world start to magically show up. I can't tell you how many times I've been asked to write books and create programs. This didn't come about through strife and struggle; it came about because I was so immersed in my desire to share healing with others that I found myself living on the same wavelength as those opportunities. (This is how manifestation works, in case you were wondering!)

If there's any doubt or confusion when it comes to your purpose, it's helpful to think about who you were as a child, as well as the natural gifts you expressed. When I look back on my early experiences, I recall crying alone in my room and writing in my journal, "I don't know who I'm crying for, but it's not for me." At the tender age of seven, I could literally feel myself transmuting the pain and suffering of someone else on the planet with my tears. I didn't feel sad—I felt uplifted. And I had no idea what was happening, but I knew it was real. Decades later I would realize that my energy work occurs through my tears. When I'm helping someone to heal, my eyes naturally water. What I came to understand intellectually was something that the trusting, open part of my child self already knew.

Every single one of us has a gift, or several gifts, we are meant to share wholeheartedly with the world. The innocent part of us that's always connected to the light of the divine can help to reacquaint us with our purpose so that we're authentically connected to it at all times.

## PRACTICE: ACCESS YOUR GIFTS AND PURPOSE

1. What do you think your purpose is?

   a. If you don't know what your purpose is, think about what you loved doing as a child or what you want the world to feel. What came to you effortlessly? Follow the breadcrumbs, as this is vital information that will help you to move into that frequency. Remember that your purpose can be absolutely anything—it can never be too big or small.

So, don't feel pressured to turn your purpose into something that seems "significant." Through the eyes of the divine, whatever brings joy and lifts others to a high vibration is significant, no matter what form it takes!

b. Often, we can get some insight about the special gifts that fuel our purpose when we pay attention to energies we learned to shut off at a young age. For example, perhaps we were shamed for being "overly emotional" or punished for our irrepressible curiosity. Think of the places where you tend to hold back on fully expressing yourself, because it probably means there's a gift you're consciously or unconsciously repressing.

c. Try not to be mechanical or limit your purpose to a role or something you want to achieve. Don't just say, "I want to be an artist," or, "I want to cure cancer." A purpose is less about what you're doing and more about who you're being. Get into the deep, core feelings that are connected to whatever lights you up. Instead of focusing on yourself, focus on how you want the world to feel.

2. If you aren't fully living your purpose, what do you feel is holding you back?

a. Write out a list of all the "reasons" you can't live in your purpose. They might look like, "I don't have the time," "I don't have the money," "I don't know if other people will care about what I'm doing." Let loose and write down whatever comes to mind.

b.  Now, look at your list. Identify
how each of these reasons might be
a manifestation of your limiting
human story.

3.  Think of the person you would embody if you
were accessing and using all your gifts to help
others. What kinds of qualities would you
be expressing? (Love, gratitude, joy, beauty,
compassion, deep listening, etc.)

4.  Next, rewrite your purpose as an "embodied"
statement. That might look like: "I'm
embodying absolute compassion and
acceptance for the people I encounter, whatever
they're going through."

5.  Instead of waiting for the "right" moment
or believing that you have to live out your
purpose in a big and dramatic way, choose
to consciously embody that purpose. Start
small, in your own backyard. On a daily
basis, intentionally take the time to embody
your most purposeful self. Don't fixate on the
business you feel intimidated about starting,
or all the "action steps" you think you need
to take to get there; build your purpose into
your dominant reality by letting the qualities
associated with it flow through your body, your
words, your emotions, and your interactions
with others.

6.  Embody your purpose for at least 30 days. You
might not always feel like you can step into the

soulful qualities associated with your purpose, but try your best to do this every day. Take time to journal about the magical occurrences that will absolutely take place when you step into your purpose.

## YOUR DIVINE LIGHT PRACTICE

Repeat the steps of the *Access Your Gifts and Purpose* practice. If you feel uncertain about your purpose, spend extra time on the first step. Sometimes, our greatest dreams have been shamed into hiding, but with gentleness and persistence, it's possible to coax them back to the surface.

As always, take time to revisit the reflection questions at the end of each section in this chapter, and to journal on them.

### Takeaways

1. The fifth pathway of light, **transmutation**, is the process of changing from a low-vibration state to a high-vibration one. Every time we're willing to transmute our pain for the purpose of connecting with the divine and being our authentic selves on this planet, we magnify the light within us so that it becomes a beacon for all living beings.

2. Gift shift theory refers to the idea that a quality or aspect of our history that may once have wounded us can become our greatest gift, if we allow it to.

3. All of us use a specific "currency" to pay for the mistakes we believe we made in the past. There is nothing wrong with wanting to make amends for harmful behavior, but too often, this currency is not a high-vibration energy and comes in the form of self-hatred and self-sabotage—which doesn't end up helping us or anyone else, in the long run.

4. In transmuting a toxic relationship or situation, we make a commitment to stand in our soul. Even when it feels difficult and requires us to dispense tough love, standing in our soul means we'll always act in the interest of the highest good for all who are involved.

5. It isn't true that most of us don't know our purpose—we usually already do, but we've been using our human story as a smokescreen that keeps us from fully stepping into it. However, instead of getting caught up in our fears about what we need to do to catalyze our purpose, we can learn to embrace it in the here and now by fully feeling and embodying it even in our smallest interactions with the world.

# CHAPTER 6

# co-creation

One thing that should be evident to you by now, especially after the last chapter, is that purpose speaks to us in breadcrumbs, just like the divine. We come to the path of light through synchronicities and other seemingly magical events. As we start to pay attention and walk toward the light, new opportunities show up that leave us marveling. This was so important for me to recognize on my own journey of spiritual growth. In the past, I couldn't comprehend that there was a way for me to have a beautiful life. I didn't believe I had the practical tools or knowledge to make it happen, but that's because I was living in my head—in the realm of, "To get from point A to point B, you have to walk a straight line." But in the realm of the divine, miracles happen, time gets bendy, and the rules of the 3D world don't really apply. The path of light is all about stepping into the heart, with an attitude of faith and surrender. This is how we begin to accept that we're partners in a divine process of **co-creation**, which is the sixth pathway of light and the subject of this chapter.

When you let your heart lead, opportunities you couldn't possibly dream of start to emerge. Even today, I'm excited about what might come tomorrow. I am aware that as far as I've come, there's growth I will experience that will give me the foundation to do even more than I'm doing now.

Of course, there's a nasty culprit that can often keep us playing small in our lives, and it's the phenomenon known as imposter syndrome, a well-studied psychological disorder in which people (usually women) doubt they have the skill, talent, or experience to accomplish what they want to accomplish. Even if they have lots of achievements under their belt, the fear of being "found out" as a fraud continues to persist. Sadly, so many incredible, beautiful souls suffer from imposter syndrome, which keeps them from sharing their gifts with the world. And if there's one thing I know for sure, it's that the divine wants you to share your gifts, your unique light, with as many beings on this planet as possible.

I often tell the coaches I train who reveal their fear of not being good enough, "Based on where you are today, there are absolutely things you can do to help others and make the world a better place. But there will always be more to learn tomorrow. Don't worry about what you don't know. Learn about yourself and step into your light a bit more every day, so that you can gradually expand into that future version of you."

I brought my son with me to a mastermind event I was holding in Sedona. My mom, who lives in Phoenix, decided that she'd come to Sedona to pick up my son so he could spend time with family. However, the night Mom came to pick up my son, he broke his arm, so we were at the hospital until 3 A.M. I had to be up at 8 A.M. to teach. Through a human lens, the entire situation was chaotic and as far from the light as one might imagine.

Mom decided to stay with me to take care of my son. As we went on a hike later that morning, she turned to me and said, "I'm so sorry that nothing went as expected. You're here serving your clients, and I'm sure it's such an inconvenience to have me here—one extra person to pay for." I looked at her in shock. None of what she'd said had even crossed my mind. Instead, I was thrilled that my students would get to meet my mom, whom I loved so much. I also felt everything that had happened was a great lesson for my masterminders about surrendering control and welcoming outcomes much grander than they might have constructed on their own. Not to mention, I was so happy that I actually felt energized rather than drained from the night before.

So, you might be wondering what any of this has to do with co-creation. The answer is: everything! Mom remembered me as the old version of me, who would most certainly have freaked out at the dramatic change in plans. But in the moment when she turned to me, thinking I was disappointed and drained by how things had turned out, I realized just how much I had grown. I'd come to see myself not as a separate little being, going through the ins and outs of life and being invariably disappointed with what happened. Instead, I knew I was a co-creator; I had a choice to surrender to every moment, not just the ones that went the way I thought they should go! Those were my mind's desires anyhow, and my heart, which speaks directly to the divine, knows better. Through surrender, I often discover that life is always working for me, not against me—but it's always up to me to find the silver lining and keep walking steadfastly toward the light, which hides all kinds of blessings I can't necessarily predict!

Your life may look far from beautiful, but stick with me here and let's start parting the clouds together. Co-creation is about seeing the miracles in the mundane—finding the intentional creation that exists in all things and seeking to understand "why" it exists—that is, "why" life might be happening for you even if you can't immediately see it. As you do this, you shift to a better "next" moment, which takes you to an optimal space of co-creation. So, the work is in shifting and expanding the perspective of what you view as "against you" and finding the harmony and connection within it.

Co-creation is
about seeing the
miracles in the
mundane.

## FEAR OF LETTING THE DIVINE TAKE THE LEAD

When you're co-creating with the divine, you're the co-pilot and you're letting the divine take the lead. At our core essence, we're no different from the divine, so you can view this as, "I'm letting my soul/higher self take the lead." This is an extraordinary shift, because it means that even if we tend to exert control in our lives (I'm looking at my type A readers here—I see you, I love you, and I totally understand you!), we can allow ourselves to walk toward divine light, which is eternally wise and knows who we truly are and what we truly want better than our human self does!

Lots of people are anxious about the idea of letting the divine take the lead. I often hear such questions as, "Will my husband still love me? Will I have to leave my job?" The message that is buried in such questions is the idea that growth is hard or that it's lonely at the summit of the mountain. This couldn't be more untrue. Certainly, when I went through major shifts, there were lots of structures that got torn down in my life, and plenty of people who dropped off. The human perception of such changes is that they signify painful loss. But, there's a future version of us that we're co-creating with the divine, and it has the power to roll with the punches and handle everything that occurs with a beautiful energy of grace and acceptance. This aspect of us, which gets birthed as we move into the light, is able to flow with the changes—because they're connected to the deeper, eternal truth of who we are. And the deepest essence of who we are is oriented toward growth and expansion, which is viewed as a welcome adventure rather than a reason to bury our heads in the sand and stay stuck in the same old, same old.

I've had moments when I was stuck in my human story and said to myself, "I don't wanna grow—it's triggering my issues around abandonment and loss!" But there was another part of me that understood I was co-creating with a higher power that wanted the best for me and that was deeply invested in my happiness. Was I happy in those times when I felt paralyzed by the fear of change? No! I was simply reverting to old patterns that felt "safe" and familiar. As I started to think about the possibility of living a life in which I felt inauthentic, I understood that my unhappiness would only make me feel emptier and more unfulfilled if I didn't lean into change and let the divine take the lead with me riding shotgun.

I started to realize that even when I lost a relationship or when I chose to step away from a particular person or situation, it wasn't really a loss. In fact, I was moving toward something that was more authentic and fulfilling. Even in the times when I had to cut off certain relationships, I knew we were still connected on a soul level and that I was leaving the door open for a different kind of relationship with that person in the future. As I've seen countless times, there's no such thing as the "end" of a relationship when we are operating on the understanding that light always brings us home to one another, even if that's only on a soul level. (Plus, we are all deeply connected, so it would not behoove me to attempt to fully disconnect from someone without taking a higher version of them into account and creating connection on that level!) As I experienced with my mom, putting the past behind us and stepping into the light meant we were able to create a brand-new relationship from the ashes of the old one. It was a relationship we both wanted and could cherish; I just had to step out of the pattern of the old one to make room for the new.

So often, the unconscious contracts we make with other people are based on trauma bonding, where you have two inauthentic and unhealed parts dancing with each other. It isn't that love doesn't exist in such relationships, but as is often the case, it's not possible to fully be yourself and step into your divine light. In such a relationship, the human perception is that it's not acceptable to be the real you—but when two people heal, they start to see each other in a new light . . . the way Mom and I did. I've had this happen with other people, as well. It is possible to welcome people back into your life, as long as you're both unburdened by the past because you've stepped into a new, lighter version of yourself.

I often find that when people are willing to do away with their reservations about letting God take the lead, it's usually because they're unhappy with some aspect of their lives. That's why so many people often get on the spiritual path when they learn about manifestation. However, the way people manifest is still too often tied to a fear-based paradigm.

Here's what I mean by that: co-creation is a principle that takes us completely beyond the human idea that we are separate, autonomous entities floating around in a world where we have to fight for power and control. When we move into the paradigm of co-creation, we're already in collaboration with the divine because we've always been connected. This is an important aspect of any kind of manifestation work: there's an interconnectedness that must be honored if we are to create anything of meaning and significance. When we see ourselves as separate beings with desires that have nothing to do with anyone else but us, our "magic" is severely limited—because the paradigm of separation is rooted in fear.

Every time I set manifestation in motion, I take time to really think about what it is I "want." Is my desire coming from a self-serving place, or is it meant to be of benefit to all the beings I'm connected to? When we look at creating, we want to ensure that our desires further a sense of connection and collaboration rather than separation. To that end, I often add, "For the highest good of all," every time I manifest. Of course, manifestation is ultimately about being in complete alignment with our beliefs, so even if our beliefs are totally rotten, manifestation can still work to our benefit. When we choose to manifest in alignment with the principle of divine co-creation, however, we are intentionally using our desires to move into the light and into integrity with our higher self.

When we co-create, we walk with the flow of existence, for the highest good of all. This is the power of letting the divine take the lead—it moves us beyond our tiny human story so we can finally recognize we're all fractals of the big shebang: the divine. With the divine as our co-pilot, we ensure that everybody wins, and that we all win consistently. The most beautiful manifestations bring us back into this state of oneness.

## Reflection Questions

1.  Consider what it would be like to let the divine take the lead in your life. What kinds of fears or excitement does that bring up in you?

2. Are there any areas of your life where you are afraid of dramatic change? What is your human story telling you? If you shift into the light of your divine story, how does that change your perspective?

3. Do you tend to see yourself as separate from the divine and all of creation? How might this be impacting your manifestations and co-creations in the world?

4. What comes up when you think about using the phrase "for the highest good of all" in your own manifestation and co-creation work?

## BALANCING SURRENDER AND WILLPOWER

When it comes to co-creation, we are not expected to be "perfect" (yes, I know I keep saying this—and that's because it's super important!) or know absolutely everything—neither do we need to do a lot of backbreaking self-improvement work.

I've heard people say they feel overwhelmed by the prospect of leading a life that's intrinsically connected to the divine, because their desired destination seems too far away (not to mention, at times, far-fetched). How can they possibly get there by willpower alone? How can they do all the work that's required?

Incredibly, co-creation is not just about using our willpower to get to our desired destination. The divine doesn't say, "Here are steps one through a hundred—now, get to work!" It only ever gives us as much as we can handle, which usually means one to three steps at a time. Instead of throwing the big picture and all the tiny details of what needs to be done at us—which would probably freak us out and stop us in our tracks—the divine gives us just the right amount of information we need. When we take one step at a time in a flow state that lets us be fully present, this actually creates a quantum leap that carries us toward what we want. Following the breadcrumbs of the divine, which is always there to support us, also brings us into alignment with our most authentic desires.

When we connect with the divine through sincere questions like, "Who am I here to be? What am I here to do? How did my human story prepare me for whatever lies ahead? How can I take some of the pressure off my perception of these things?" we co-create from our authenticity instead of getting fixated on ego-based ideas about who we should be, or what we should aspire to. We come to see that, yes, it requires action, and perhaps some realignment with our soulful needs, but it does not have to be a heavy and arduous journey. And if you believe in the magic of the divine, it will help you to recognize signs and synchronicities and to distinguish between true guidance and the ego.

When I look back on the times I simply surrendered to the divine, even if it meant I had to release something that was valuable to my human self, I can unequivocally say that the rewards on the other side were monumental. Today, I rest assured that all I have to do is live in the light and remember that I am not separate from the divine, and I will feel supported every step of the way.

However, many of us are fearful of surrender, which often comes with the mistaken belief that "I did it all by myself, and I don't need to depend on God or a higher power to do it for me." This is the result of a misunderstanding from an unhealed part of the self, which continues to see things in an oppositional way rather than recognizing we're all interconnected. Usually, the unhealed part has trust issues that need to be resolved. Even if someone is insistent that they have everything they need to take care of themselves, the underlying message is often, "I don't believe in God," or, "I can't trust that God actually cares for me."

When I encounter people who have these underlying beliefs, I offer them a great deal of compassion and validate their feelings. "You don't have to let God take the lead if you're not ready," I say.

My old staff member, Regina, was an avowed atheist who was accustomed to hearing me talk about the divine. She harbored a great deal of trauma from her childhood, as her family was deeply and dogmatically religious. I completely understood why she was so adamant about not going anywhere near the divine, as she was looking at it from the lens of her traumatic human story. I also knew that the door would be open as soon as she found a pathway into the divine that made sense to her. I never told her, "Hey, you should take a course on manifestation!" I knew it was more important for her to see an actual embodiment of the divine, so I offered her as much love and acceptance as I could. Over time, she experienced a change of heart, because she came to a relationship with the God of her own understanding.

Regina is a prime example of why it's not a great idea to proselytize to anyone. It's way more effective when people come to terms with their feelings about the divine in their own unique way. I will always do my best to shine a light on what is possible, but everyone has the free will to do whatever they want with that information.

I'm a huge proponent of surrender as a direct pathway to the light, but I am not suggesting you become entirely dependent on God, which is what some religions and spiritual systems teach. Remember that the division between you and the divine is a false one—and when you surrender, you are surrendering to the part of yourself that is inextricably connected to the divine. Dependence on God is usually framed within the paradigm that God is a bearded man in the sky (or whatever the chosen personification might look like) who's going to protect you from the big bad world and take care of everything. This is a spiritualized form of codependency, where one partner sacrifices their needs and well-being to maintain a relationship. In truth, when we surrender, we step into even more of our authentic power and truth. Our capacity to make healthy decisions grows. Sure, we operate from a place of humility and awe, but this doesn't mean that we grovel or erase ourselves in the process of connecting with the light within. Surrender moves us from a victim mentality to one that helps us become clear channels for divine messages.

A lot of people I meet start out in self-development from a place of giving their energy and power away. Sometimes, their power is their currency: if they give it away to a guru or someone who seems to have everything figured out, that person will solve their problems. And if they surrender to God, God will rain down blessings. This is a false relationship, because it frames our connection with the divine in a very human and transactional way. The divine doesn't need you to be "less than" to love and connect with you; the divine just wants you to be open to recognizing the light and making the decision to walk toward it.

I also come across people who were indoctrinated into a very religious way of thinking about God, and who might view the divine as an omniscient father figure. While there's nothing wrong with this (and it can be comforting to develop our own personal relationship with the divine), it does cause me to wonder how such a person relates to their own father or parents. And if they have children, how do they relate to them? Is there a sense of freedom and acceptance in the relationship, or is it bound by obedience or the need to sacrifice one's personal truth to keep the peace? Is there respect for the fact that we live in a freewill universe, and that even if the "parental" figure isn't obeyed, the "child" in the relationship will still be loved and supported?

When there's mutual respect and a sense of "we're all in this together," surrender and willpower begin to work in a more symbiotic way. Surrender is amazing when it comes to the realization that there are certain things we just can't try to "logic" our way through. In many of my own creative endeavors, I'd feel totally overwhelmed if I attempted to plot everything out in a nuts-and-bolts type of way. When I accept the breadcrumbs that the divine is sending down to me, I can accept that I'll find a way through, even if I don't know the path in advance. Surrender shoots us back into pure possibility and helps us recognize that the journey is an important part of the process. We can chill out on the white-knuckling and give ourselves more space and grace to do what needs to be done.

This makes us more available to make solid decisions when we need to—to use our wonderful, rational, human brain to translate the guidance of the divine into positive action. This is how we begin to master our own lives and to get into a flow that allows us to embrace our true power. It changes the way we "do" co-creation, because it breaks down the false construct that places the divine way above our heads as an inaccessible paragon of power. If we are no longer separate from the divine, surrender and personal willpower don't have to be leagues apart. In fact, our willpower can become an extension of the divine—a way that we choose to locate and express our light in the world.

## Reflection Questions

1. Do you feel you have to work hard in your life to accomplish anything? How has this belief supported you? And how might this mentality be holding you back from stepping into the light?

2. Have there been times when you've felt disappointed in or mistrustful of the divine? What is the story behind this resistance? Can you gently recognize the places where you may have developed distorted or incomplete beliefs about the divine that make it difficult to practice surrender?

3. On the other end of the spectrum, have there ever been times when you were overly dependent on the divine? In what ways might you have given your true power away to feel taken care of?

4. How might surrender and willpower come together to support your divine co-creations?

## PLAYING THE HUMAN GAME
## VS. THE ENERGY GAME

The human game is full of steps and how-tos—templates for getting from point A to point B. As many people who've utilized this as a path to self-improvement can attest, taking this prefabricated route gets you to the top of the leaderboard about 50 percent of the time. But when we shift into the light, we begin to play the energy game; that is, we start to see an array of infinite possibilities and paths to get to the feeling of the divine—which, whether we realize it or not, is our soul's deepest yearning: to feel connected to All That Is.

When we play the energy game, the old human rules go out the window. Time is no longer linear and predictable, and things can turn on a dime. Even though we might receive information about what's next in the form of breadcrumbs, we discover that we have the capacity to move faster than the speed of light and to get to our destination that much more quickly. That's the magic of co-creation. And when we realize that co-creation is a game that takes place in the realm of energy, we begin to take quantum leaps in our growth.

When Oliver and I feel stuck inside a problem we can't seem to solve, we automatically ask ourselves if we're playing the human game or the energy game. Generally, if things feel heavy, confusing, or foggy, we understand that we're probably not in the right vibration to approach the issue, meaning it's time to shift gears so we can play the energy game. The way we do this is, we begin to discuss completely unrelated topics that allow us to shift into a mindset of feeling positive, enthusiastic, and awe-inspired. It's a lot like going on a walk or taking a nap to get your mind off a nagging problem—and then, suddenly, in the middle of a dream or while you're out on a trail in the woods, the solution comes surging toward you.

When you shift into a higher vibration—of relaxation, beauty, peace, calm—you seldom have to go searching for solutions. In fact, they tend to fall right into your lap . . . but only when you stop trying to win the human game and come back to—you guessed it!—a place of surrender and simplicity. This carries you through seemingly difficult times because it broadens your perspective and allows you to navigate the twists and turns with greater ease and foresight. That's why surrender and simplicity are aspects of what I like to call the ABCs of manifesting!

Admittedly, too many of us make this way harder on ourselves than it needs to be. Many years ago, I met Alice at an event I was holding to learn all the steps of manifestation. Alice was a tough cookie with a highly active left brain. She was obviously interested in topics of a spiritual nature, but she thought she could muscle her way through with her intellect alone. During the event, she raised her hand, notebook at the ready, and asked, "When you say it's important to get into your heart, how exactly do we do that?"

I could immediately sense that Alice was in search of a method, a technique, a tried-and-true program of steps she could write down and practice whenever she needed to. This gut feeling was only validated each time Alice raised her hand to ask a question that was about finding the "right" strategy. Alice was stuck in the human game, which is paradoxically how I recognized that a series of steps wasn't the lesson she needed to learn. In fact, if I satisfied her need for certainty, she would continue to remain stuck. Part of the human game she was playing was giving her power away to a "guru" (in this case, me, even though I definitely don't aspire to such a role!), to gain the secret that would magically alleviate all her problems. But there was no energy, not even the energy of genuine desire, behind her seeking. In her mind, manifestation was a mechanical process—even though what I teach is only secondarily about manifesting results in the world and primarily about helping people step into the soul growth that is possible when they connect with the light.

I was blunt. "For you, I'm not going to offer any steps." Of course, Alice was livid when I said this. After all, wasn't that what she'd paid for?

Years later, I encountered Alice, and she was a changed person. "You know, I was really mad at first when you told me you weren't going to give me any steps. I had no idea why, and I thought you were just mad at me," she said. "But over time, I realized that the biggest lesson I had to learn was just trusting myself." When Alice finally got it, she became an instantaneous manifester. This came from being able to step into her heart—not because someone in a position of authority told her how to do it, but because she got there on her own, in her own way.

Alice went on to say, "I didn't appreciate you back then, but I get what you're doing now. You refused to let me give my power to you, and you held so much space for me! I was frustrated in the moment, but I can't even begin to tell you what you did for my life. You were so humble and patient with me, and it made a huge difference!"

The energy game is available to all of us. After all, each of us is a fractal of the divine. The answers truly *are* within, and the journey to finding them will look different for everyone.

Another great example of how people find their own way into the energy game comes from one of my students, Emma. She was a business coach who was very much in her head. Emma was ruled by her inner masculine and had a strong left brain that guided her to get things done and make money more efficiently. She enrolled in one of my masterminds because she wanted to be even more successful and to manifest greater abundance. Several months in, she came to me and said, "Want to know something funny, Mandy? When I became your student, I actually stopped doing affirmations!"

"That's interesting. Why is that?" I asked.

Emma explained, "I'd get up religiously every morning and have a routine of affirmations, but nothing I was saying ever came true! Then, I learned from you what was happening: I wasn't housing the frequency of the affirmation, so nothing was changing!" As Emma shared, her daily affirmations were pulling her further from the goal she wanted to move toward. They were just words, with zero energetic embodiment. Affirmations can be amazing tools. However, if someone chooses to do affirmations without the energy of belief supporting them, their mind will perceive whatever they're saying to be a lie, which will end up setting them back even further.

As Emma discovered on her own, when we don't feel the truth of what we're doing in our heart and body and it's all coming from our head, our life doesn't change. In most of these cases, we haven't done the inner work to determine if we actually believe what we're saying—and if we don't, to then consider why we might be holding ourselves back.

I gave Emma a new assignment: follow her intuition every morning, even with the tiniest of matters like deciding on coffee or tea, or if she preferred to work out at the gym or go for a walk that day. "Start remembering what it *feels* like to feel what you want and where you're headed," I advised. Of course, the operative word was *feel*.

Things quickly began to turn around for Emma, and she experienced healing and abundance in several areas of her life. She learned what people who play the energy game know: when you live intuitively, you have a straight shot to the divine. It's like you're on the phone with source consciousness at all times, and you begin building your muscle around knowing what's for you and what isn't. This is the essence of co-creation, and it offers a sense of pure peace and the awareness that you're receiving direct and genuine guidance. And trust me, while the guidance doesn't always make logical sense, the wisdom and truth behind it is undeniable.

When I was in the process of buying a retreat center, I thought I wanted to purchase a property in Hawaii. Through a human lens, I thought it would be so cool to have a retreat center right on the ocean, in a gorgeous tropical environment. However, for some reason, I felt called to look into properties in a tiny town in Colorado where it could snow five months out of the year. It just *felt* right! I followed my intuition to stay in a state of surrender and pure possibility, which allowed me to manifest the most incredible outcomes and discover a magical property that I fell completely in love with. I was playing the energy game all out.

Getting in touch with our intuition is a personal voyage that all of us need to figure out for ourselves. I fully get that people like specificity and concrete answers that help them wrap their mind around some of the weird and bizarre aspects of things like manifestation and energy medicine. However, the true gift of the spiritual experience is when people find their truth—without some kind of cookie-cutter technique. I can absolutely facilitate and be part of that process, but it becomes more of a call-and-response that we both get to partake in as opposed to a set of rote instructions I give them (which wouldn't be very fun, anyway). During my workshops and events, I will talk to at least a dozen people who are grappling with money issues. I'll give every single one of them a different lesson to ponder and integrate, because each root cause is totally different. It's not my job to solve their problems or tell them what to do, but to help them recognize and remove any of the obstacles in their path that are keeping them from the joy and possibility that are part of the energy game. My aim is to give them only the amount of information that will help them get onto that totally different playing field on their own. This helps them develop their own co-creative relationship with the divine, while keeping their inner power intact.

The energy game is never one-size-fits-all. It's kind of like a video game with infinite characters and infinite narrative arcs that can't necessarily be predicted. Every single one of us is truly a unique snowflake. We have our similarities, but the energy game allows us to embrace our beautiful differences. Divinely speaking, each of us is already divine and perfect, exactly as we are. An important aspect of this wild roller-coaster ride we're on is to find that out for ourselves.

**Reflection Questions**

1.  In what ways are you playing the human game and searching for a set of instructions or techniques that will get you to where you need to go? How has that impacted your life, positively or negatively?

2. When you think about stepping into the energy game, how does that make you feel? Is there any resistance that comes up? If so, how can you begin to embrace surrender and simplicity instead?

3. In what ways can you begin using your intuition to receive divine guidance and embody the energy of abundance, peace, flow, and light?

4. The next time you feel frustrated by the sense that the "rules" for achieving what you want to achieve are elusive, how might you shift from seeing this as an obstacle to seeing it as a beautiful opportunity to step into the energy game?

## MIRACLES AND DIVINE INTERVENTION

We can't talk about co-creation without talking about the presence of miracles and what some might call "divine intervention." In truth, I don't really believe that the divine "intervenes" to change our lives. It's more that we get glimpses of the light, and even the tiniest slivers of that light connect us to the divine story, which is vast and magical. As I lean further into my light, a series of occurrences opens up that just don't seem logical when looked at head-on. But this, too, is an aspect of co-creation rather than something that can be attributed to supernatural causes. You can think of it this way: we're always manifesting (and countermanifesting, which, if you remember, is the process by which you manifest from a troubled unconscious mind rather than a clear conscious mind), and we're always in conversation with the universe. Miracles occur when that conversation happens in an open way that allows us to actually pay attention to the responses we're getting!

Here's the beautiful thing: We don't necessarily have to be happy, peaceful, joyful, and in our highest vibration to experience miracles. We just have to be open to the fact that there is a better way than the one we've found ourselves resorting to. This is why there are so many incredible stories about human beings who are "saved by angels" during their lowest hours. In most cases, such people are totally in the now, in a surrendered state that welcomes flashes of insightful knowing and things that can't be explained by logic or the human story.

Many years ago, back when I was in the midst of my own dark night of the soul and felt like I was at my lowest point, as if the light within me was completely turned off, I hit surrender. From that point, my life flipped upside down. Oliver messaged me, and for the first time in my life, I found myself in a healthy and loving relationship where I felt like I could step into a higher version of myself. A series of other things occurred. It was as if my future self had swooped in to show me what was possible. The energetic shift that occurred was not owing to the person I was, as no version of me that existed could have created such incredible miracles. This was "divine intervention" in full-throttle action.

Since then, the incredible events (often, ones that occurred "at just the right moment") have continued to pour into my life. These have included things like being sent seed money for my philanthropic work, or meeting people who led me to the next opportunities in love, life, and business. All of this has happened too often to chalk it up to random coincidence. Miracles are forms of synchronicity that indicate there's an invisible yet palpable web of connection that exists between all people, places, and phenomena. When we tap into that with our pure intention and full surrender, anything is possible. When something in my life just isn't working, I inquire as to whether I'm in a state of genuine surrender; if not, that's where I go to tap back into a state of pure possibility.

But again, we have to be open to miracles in order for us to even notice they're happening—because, yes, some miracles might seem small or like we're just making them up. But when we greet them with an attitude of authentic gratitude, wonder, and awe, we are basically opening the portal that will take us directly into the light, into the dimension of the highest vibration (no space travel or time machine necessary!). This is by no means a passive process—it requires your active, full participation! You can't be a passive bystander in your life; you are here to be part of the human experience, but it's also your job to be on the lookout for the divine, which will always provide the light we're all looking for in the midst of the darkness.

Some of my favorite stories about miracles come from the people in my community, many of whom find me at the lowest moments in their lives. I've heard so many stories about how they surrendered and prayed for a miracle. A woman named Naomi recently shared with me how she'd been in an ongoing struggle with anxiety, every day, for years. "When I thought of the future, fear and worry would fill my mind," she said. "I would often go into negative downward spirals of thoughts and emotions and would stay there for days, not knowing how to get out of it. I was tired of living this way, I was tired of struggling, I was tired of feeling anxious—I was just done with life in general. I grew up going to church, loving God, loving others, and trying my best. But this world just has such a heavy weight. All I wanted was to be free of this feeling of being stuck. I just wanted to be at peace. But how?"

Naomi was scrolling through social media one day in an attempt to numb her anxiety when she found a video in which I shared tips on how to raise one's vibration, something she'd never heard of. She clicked on a link for an upcoming three-day event I was holding, and although she didn't know exactly what it was all about, she followed her gut and signed up for it. Since that event, Naomi's life changed. Within weeks, she signed up for one of my coaching courses, although becoming a coach had been the furthest thing from her mind. "I had never invested in myself before, so I was taking a big leap of faith and decided to start my self-growth journey."

Naomi used the tools I taught to become focused on learning how to love herself and rewrite her human story, which was riddled with limiting thoughts and beliefs. She was skeptical at first, but she was willing to try. "Day by day, my mind was expanding, my heart was expanding—little did I know I was starting the process of turning from a caterpillar into a butterfly."

For Naomi, the process was subtle, but the shift was dramatic. "When change happens little by little, it is sometimes hard to see your progress. But one night, a few months after my journey started, I lay my head on my pillow and tears of gratitude filled my eyes as I realized I hadn't said anything negative about myself that day. I began to see the beauty in each day. The amazing ground-ing feeling of walking on the earth barefoot. The beauty of going for a swim in the ocean and putting my toes in the sand. As I raised my vibration, each day seemed to be filled with magical little moments. I started to see repeating numbers like 1:11, 2:22, 3:33, 4:44, and 5:55 on clocks, on signs, on my odometer, and all around me. I started to feel divine guidance, I started trusting my intuition, and amazing little miracles seemed to be happening to me almost daily."

Naomi became more comfortable asking the divine for signs that she was heading in the right direction by pursuing coaching, which was a brand-new passion that seemed to have emerged out of nowhere. One day, when she did this, she got full-body tingles and looked up into the sky to see a bald eagle circling overhead. She asked the divine if this was the sign she'd asked for, only to see another bald eagle appear before her eyes. "They circled above me, dancing on the wind, and tears of gratitude filled my eyes. Now, I see bald eagles often when I ask for guidance, both in real life, and on stickers, books, TV, signs, and sides of trucks and billboards! One day I was driving along and an inspired thought entered my mind. I asked, 'God, is this from you? Should I do this?' Moments later, I looked out my window, and there was a massive semi truck driving beside me with the biggest eagle head on it I've ever seen! I couldn't believe my eyes! I just laughed and laughed with joy because I never thought in a million years that life could be this magical."

Naomi learned, as many do, that the divine speaks in signs and symbols, and the bald eagle became her surefire way of recognizing missives that came directly from the realm of spirit. This experience of direct interaction with God filled her with a joy that was infectious and bubbled into her work with other people. She came to a place where she could honestly say that she completely loves and accepts herself. She takes this sense of innate peace and freedom into her work with others, to inspire them and let them know they aren't alone.

Miracles can put us directly in touch with our purpose, and they can also liberate us from legacies of trauma and disconnection. Sujuan is a Chinese woman who grew up in a poor family. She had an older brother, and ever since childhood, she felt that her family's culture placed more value on boys than girls. Sujuan felt neglected by her family, while her brother was held up as the golden child. Her mother was overly critical toward her, which ended up making Sujuan rebellious and angry; this continued into her adult years.

Sujuan told me, "After my son was born three years ago, I didn't talk to my mom for a whole year, as I felt so unloved by her compared to my brother. I couldn't imagine how a parent could treat their child that way, especially after I became a mom. I told myself that she didn't deserve my love . . . but I wasn't happy. An inner part of me wanted to change."

Like Naomi, Sujuan decided to join one of my programs, which helped her to see her mom in a different light—through the eyes of empathy. "I started to understand how tough it was for her to raise two children in a challenging environment. Our family was in such a poor financial state that we didn't have a flushing toilet until my 20s." She also had her programming that was passed down to her from her parents, the culture, and society.

A dinner with a childhood friend helped Sujuan's relationship with her mother as well. They weren't close friends, but Sujuan had the sense that he was a wise man. "When he called us to come to his home, the time was 4:44 P.M. When we arrived at his home, my phone showed 5:55 P.M. His car's license plate had the exact four digits with my cellphone number." Throughout recorded history, certain numbers have been associated with miracles, and Sujuan's ability to take notice of this clued her into the fact that something was about to change.

She said, "Later that night, I had the worst trigger with my mom. I wanted to pack my clothes and leave her place right away. Then, I thought of the wise friend. So many signs showed me that this friend might help me with my relationship with my mom. Following my intuition and not overthinking how strange it was to talk with him about something so embarrassing, I called him and told him my story. He told me my mom's story through his eyes, offering a neutral and different perspective. At that moment, I began to see my whole life and my mom's through a different lens: our divine stories. Because I held so much anger and resentment, I couldn't see how much she loves me. The idea that she cared more for my brother than me is another limiting belief. Though she didn't love me the way I expected, she has loved me as best as she can. Today, my mom teaches me compassion and forgiveness. I teach her love."

Sujuan's experience with her mother was the beginning of a new life chapter filled with love, peace, and joy. The human story and game tends to condition us with the belief that transformation, especially in historically painful relationships, can take years or even lifetimes to resolve. Sujuan was astounded to see her relationship with her mother shift within a matter of days and weeks. But it was her ability to trust her intuition (another divinely given gift that connects us to our light when we take the time to listen to it!) that led her home to herself.

She said it best when she proclaimed, "I believe that when we tap into our authentic self and follow our divine intuition, everything unfolds beautifully!"

## Reflection Questions

1. Do you believe in miracles? If not, what are the limiting beliefs that keep you from recognizing or welcoming them? If so, what are some of the experiences you've had that have helped you to feel more connected to the divine?

2. How often do you listen to and follow your intuition? In the times when you've been intentional about following it, what has happened? When you chose not to follow it, what were the consequences?

3. Have you experienced specific signs and synchronicities (e.g., the presence of a specific bird, like Naomi's bald eagle, or series of numbers, like the ones Sujuan encountered) that alerted you to the presence of the divine and gave you a signal to move toward the light?

4. The next time you encounter a challenge or major question you need answers to, can you remember to ask for a sign—from a place of surrender rather than one of anxiety and the need to exert control? When you do, be sure to record your answers; the more you take time to pay attention to what's happening, the clearer your communication with the divine will be. But please be patient with yourself throughout this process, and don't worry about getting an answer within a certain time period. The need for specific answers at a specific

time means you've jumped back into control. Gently remind yourself to reenter the space of surrender. The frequency of surrender doesn't yearn for an answer and doesn't look at time constraints, so you will know if you are in the right space based on your "need to know."

## GROW 1 PERCENT EVERY DAY
## BY MANAGING YOUR TRIGGERS

As you've already seen, co-creation takes us into the new version of ourselves, the one that naturally brings us deeper into the heart of the light we are. This can happen in an instant, and it can also be a process that takes time. But true soul growth is not about comparing ourselves to anyone else. It is about getting really honest with ourselves, in the way that Naomi and Sujuan were able to, and to recognize that something about our current path isn't working. This is not meant to be an invalidating judgment, but information that allows us to move forward. Our emotional honesty is what helps us to perceive ourselves with greater clarity. When we begin to clear out the limiting beliefs that have kept us stuck, we create a "void" inside our mind and an energetic field that allows the light to come rushing in.

Here's the great thing: It's not about growing 100 percent and completely shifting our perception of who we are at an identity level. All we have to do is grow 1 percent; maybe we're not doing this every single day, but we're doing it consistently and progressively. Trust me that it builds over time! And if any of this sounds at all overwhelming, please be assured that it's just a molehill you get to step over. You've probably built it up as a mountain in your mind, but often, the things that take us into dramatic transformation are quite small when we look at them clearly. Often, these "tiny" things become obstacles in our perception, but once they're out of the way, we free up our energy massively and our perception naturally transforms—which means, so does our entire life. That means you can shrink down the proverbial mountain as you joyfully enter the process of growth. Be assured that if you intentionally focus on even just a little bit of growth and self-reflection on a daily basis, you are moving further into the light.

I also want to clarify that growing 1 percent every day isn't ultimately about "changing" who you are or trying to emulate someone you admire who you think is operating at a high vibration. (Remember, comparison is part of the human game, not the energy game!) It's about moving into the most authentic and natural version of yourself— the *you* you came to the planet naturally being. Just like with my work around manifestation, my focus is on helping people to figure out what's stopping them from manifesting. What are they countermanifesting and bringing into existence without even realizing it? What in their life is clashing with what they say they want, most likely due to an unconscious fear? It's my goal to help them identify those things, so that they have what they need in order to automatically let their light shine and be who they've always been—a radiant ray of the divine in human form.

All of us have the experience of getting triggered by our human story and falling out of the divine story; another way of saying this is that we might get immersed in the dark clouds to the extent that we forget the light of the sun. The clouds will come and go, but true growth is about knowing our divine nature at all times, even when we aren't necessarily surrounded by rainbows. Sometimes, our growth lessons can be downright challenging, but they will help us to reframe the things that trigger us if we open our hearts and remember that the divine is always supporting us, even if—like the sun hiding behind the clouds—we can't immediately see it.

These days, I welcome my triggers—seriously! I used to view triggers as stimuli that threw me out of my divine light, but today, I look at it in a different way. Triggers are giving me powerful feedback about the things I need to understand in order to heal; and when I heal, I expand and life becomes even more exciting. In this way, I've learned to greet growth not as a painful necessity, but as something beautiful that reaps massive rewards. Besides, as we discussed in Chapter 4, an emotional experience can't last in the body longer than 90 seconds—after that, we're making a choice to stay there!

I often tell people, "It's not the trigger that caused the emotion—but the meaning you placed on that trigger." So, growth can be as simple as remembering this and taking into account the story you're telling yourself about this trigger. This is where it's powerful to use a *pattern interrupt*, which I define as anything that shifts your emotions and redirects your energy when you react negatively to a trigger. In order not to dip back down into the dense human story, you have to interrupt that flow of energy. You can begin managing your triggers on a daily basis, rather than getting whipped around and inundated by your human story. Moving into a high vibration isn't about summoning some kind of otherworldly magic or forcing an unnatural state. It can be as mundane as lovingly desensitizing your triggers and learning to meet the needs of your unhealed parts. When you do this, your brain will rewire itself over time and your entire perspective will change.

This is how you can use 3D consciousness to support the process of co-creation. You will discover, without a doubt, that as you grow, the divine will come rushing in to fill the void of your old beliefs. You will find yourself truly living in the light.

## PRACTICE: GROW 1 PERCENT EVERY DAY BY MANAGING YOUR TRIGGERS

1. Take a moment to bring to your mind (but even more so, your heart!) a trigger that has recently come up for you. Don't choose the one that's the strongest or that feels the most destabilizing. Instead, go for something simple, like being annoyed by your partner or feeling snubbed by a friend who abruptly ended a conversation. Start small and build your capacity for working with more complex or difficult triggers.

2. Now, for a moment, welcome and accept that this trigger is only coming up because there's an unhealed part of you that wants your attention. Instead of getting seduced by all the thoughts and feelings associated with it, remind yourself to stay curious and neutral.

3. Ask yourself: *What am I telling myself about this trigger?* This doesn't mean getting wrapped up in all the feelings and stories associated with it, which can often lead to the shame and blame game. Instead, be with whatever the trigger is

bringing up. What is the feedback it's giving you about how you've chosen to identify with it? For example, you might say, "My partner gave me a weird look that set me off. If I look deeper into that, I know it set me off because I was already resonating with the idea that I'm not that attractive today. In fact, I remember waking up and feeling kind of gross when I looked in the mirror." This gentle curiosity helps us to see how and where we got hooked. The trigger might seem external, but that's only because it's connecting to an internal belief about something we incorrectly identified with. (For a reminder, go back to my story about Maggie in the STRO section of Chapter 2 and how she self-identified with the belief that she didn't belong, which is what caused her to resonate with the trigger of Dave talking over her.) Please remember to be compassionate with yourself! You might want to place your hand over your heart and breathe some loving energy into any realizations that are coming up for you.

4. It's time to do something that interrupts this unhealed part's well-meaning way of protecting you that is not currently serving you. I recommend using three different types of pattern interrupts:

   a. *Physical:* You might want to try a silly dance in the mirror or ten push-ups—anything that really gets you into your kinesthetic experience and connects you with your body, which can help interrupt any toxic mental constructs that might have seeped in.

b. *Mental/emotional:* This might look like taking time to journal, cry, make a piece of art, or do some mindfulness meditation. Our mind can be a great ally to us when we're not using it against ourselves!

c. *Spiritual:* You might choose to talk to a higher power, pray, read a spiritual book, listen to a talk by a spiritual teacher, or do anything that creates an intentional connection that helps you expand into the light.

5. Now that you've interrupted the pattern, evaluate how you feel about the trigger. Very likely, something has shifted and you're in a more neutral zone. Now that the "poison" has been neutralized (and it's okay if it doesn't feel like it's 100 percent gone), take time to journal about the need that was attached to the unhealed part. Perhaps the need was for loving connection or a sense of authentic presence from the people in your life. Even though the need was not met in this instance, how might you go about meeting that need for yourself? Remember, as you approach your unhealed parts proactively and with deep compassion, the universe will start to bring in more opportunities for you to have the very thing you're looking for!

## YOUR DIVINE LIGHT PRACTICE

Repeat the *Grow 1 Percent Every Day by Managing Your Triggers* practice. You can do this exercise with as many challenges as you wish, but start small and don't go with the most "triggering" trigger. I encourage you to come back to this exercise daily, as it will be instrumental in moving you toward the light and into a clearer channel of co-creative communication with the divine.

As always, take time to revisit the reflection questions at the end of each section in this chapter, and to journal on them.

### Takeaways

1. The sixth pathway of light, **co-creation**, helps us to remember that the divine speaks to us in breadcrumbs—and as we walk decisively toward the divine, it comes rushing toward us.

2. Often, we stall out in the process of co-creation due to a fear of surrendering and of allowing the divine to take the lead. But we can rest assured that the act of surrender isn't about giving our power away; it's about opening up to even more authenticity and joy, since the divine wants us to be fully expressed in the ways that will bring us the greatest fulfillment.

3. We can learn to balance surrender and willpower—by recognizing that we don't have to work so hard to get to our desired destination, and by recognizing that the divine

has no desire to take away our free will or sense of autonomy as we navigate life.

4. We can determine whether we're playing the human game if we're focused on a fixed "route" to getting the things we want. We know we're playing the energy game when we shift into the light and start to recognize there are infinite possibilities and paths that lead us into the light—meaning the "rules" don't apply here!

5. As we start to lean further into the light, magical synchronicities that don't seem to be logical or even possible begin to fall onto our path. However, what we think of as a "miracle" isn't something supernatural. It's just evidence that we're constantly in conversation with the universe, as miracles happen when the conversation is flowing and we're paying close attention to what the divine is telling us!

6. Co-creation is all about doing what we can in our 3D world to bring in the light. If we want to expand our capacity for dialoguing and manifesting with the universe, one of the best ways to do this is to commit to growing 1 percent on a daily basis. We can do exactly that when we commit to a practice of managing our triggers and interrupting the patterns that serve to take us out of the light.

# CHAPTER 7

# coherence

A book about finding the light within would be incomplete without the seventh and final pathway of light, which brings us full circle: **coherence**. The divine is synonymous with coherence, which is the supreme frequency of all that is. It is the thing that allows us to form a unified whole and to integrate all the different elements of our lives—including our human and divine stories. It's also what, in the therapeutic world, might be referred to as "holding space" or "embodying love." In the parlance of the HeartMath Institute, coherence can be defined as "a high-performance and healthy state—physically, emotionally, mentally and spiritually—that brings out the very best in us. The term *coherence* implies harmonious order, connectedness, stability, and efficient use of energy."

While coherence ties all the other pathways of light together because it gives us a framework for what's happening when we step into the light of our divine self, it's simultaneously the culmination of all the learning and reflection you've done so far on this journey. Coherence helps us recognize the nature of reality, and this is the kind of wisdom that changes us on a cellular level. It's also what enables us to dance within the polarities of our experience and to create heaven on earth, the way so many sages and teachers since time immemorial have taught. We attain a sense of coherence when we fully get that life is an awe-inspiring mystery, and there is so much more to it than we may initially perceive.

Coherence can also be viewed as the state of enlightenment that brings us into an unshakable sense of the foundation of existence, which is oneness. I call this the *Is*. I remember doing energy work with a friend of mine and having a moment where we synchronized completely in body, mind, and spirit. Both of us were staring at each other, unable to put into words what we were experiencing. Our husbands were in the room and were observing us, trying to make sense of what was happening. Of course, the experience defied any kind of rational explanation, even though my friend and I both tried to offer one. All I could say was, "It just *is*." This state of Is included both love and its absence, both everything and nothing. It felt neither good nor bad, and it contained all emotions and no emotion. It was a void of infinite possibility that seemed, to me, to evoke the presence of source consciousness—what I refer to as the divine.

We don't necessarily feel the presence of the Is at every moment of our lives, but as we step more and more into the light, we get more glimpses. It is truly the experience of being present with the innate complexity/simplicity of existence. Instead of being rigid about ourselves and all of life, coherence is what allows us to open up to paradox, to the extent that we start to appreciate and play with the contradictions that we hold within ourselves . . . until they are no longer contradictions but parts of a beautiful and intricate whole.

Coherence is also the end result of all the other pathways of light: that is, we embrace **expansion** by moving into the divine light, and into greater **self-knowledge** and **empathy**, so we can develop the **clarity** that is necessary to begin the process of **transmutation** of our shadows, which moves us into divine **co-creation**. All of these pathways work together to create **coherence**.

Coherence is also a quality that helps us to weave together all these different pathways so that we gain an understanding of the human realm that might not otherwise have been possible. I used to wonder how to deal with the fact that some people don't ever make it to the full expression of their divine light, due to limiting human choices. I can understand how these choices contribute to people cutting their lives short or result in them becoming shells of their former selves, but for a long time, that didn't make it any less painful to me. It was hard to see the silver lining in these human tragedies or to recognize coherence.

This is especially true when it comes to one of my dear friends from high school, Jason. Jason was a talented athlete who got involved with drugs and the wrong crowd at an early age. Eventually, the drugs consumed him to the point that he became barely functional. He was in and out of jail, and he couldn't hold down a decent job. A few years ago, Jason reached out to me for advice. As we talked, he expressed how proud he was of me for not following the same path that he and a lot of our friends had. Just last year, Jason told some of our friends that he was feeling suicidal. That same week, he coincidentally crashed his car into a wall, leaving behind a girlfriend and a beautiful daughter.

Jason could have become a professional athlete—he was that good and had so much going for him. But he didn't get to live out that particular story, because the story of his addiction swallowed that possibility. He'd gone too far down the rabbit hole to come out of it.

In retrospect, the loss didn't hit me immediately. I felt sad about it, but I'd begun to pull away from him several years before his death. I'd stepped away from those troubles altogether, and most of the people from my former life had dropped off once I stepped onto my path of light and healing. I loved Jason, but there was a part of me that had kept him at arm's length because it was difficult for me to trust people with addictive patterns, given my experience with my dad and so many others. It wasn't until I recently heard a song that reminded me of our friendship—Lil' Troy's "Wanna Be a Baller"—that the facade fell apart and I broke down crying. The song felt like an anthem for all the people I'd known, like Jason, who'd never made it. As I reminisced while I sat outside my childhood home about singing that song with friends throughout my adolescence, I held myself with the utmost compassion. "I'm so sorry, Jason," I said to myself, over and over again, as I listened to that song on repeat.

I was dealing with extreme survivor's guilt, because I was the one who'd made it out, against the odds. When I opened myself up to the reality of what I'd suppressed, however, it wasn't just an endless well of guilt and sorrow. My tears also contained the wisdom and truth of my own life journey. I hadn't been able to help Jason or my dad, or the many friends and family I lost to suicide, drugs, or jail; often, this is true when it comes to the people you love or feel closest to. My sister helped me to put this in a larger context when she said, "Jason didn't really want help, so he couldn't receive it. You can let go of the guilt."

This helped me to consider the many people who've reached out to me over the years to share things like, "I used to be suicidal, but then I went to one of your events, and because of your work and message, I'm here today." I knew then and there that it was time to change my story of survivor's guilt to a story of humility and wonder. Instead of saying, "I'm sorry, Jason," I could say, "Look what I've helped people to overcome, Jason." Because I know he'd be proud. Heck, he would have traded himself out for some of the souls I have served to ensure they'd be okay; he was that divinely loving and giving!

Today, whenever someone sends me a beautiful message sharing the ways in which my work has given them a new lease on life, it makes me smile, look up, and say, "We did it, Jason."

Even though he wasn't able to be the version of himself that was deeply connected to his divine light, he continues to indirectly fuel my desire to help people realize that they are not broken. I was also able to heal my sadness around losing him while maintaining a sense of connection to his eternal essence.

There are times when I think about him from a human perspective, I feel angry and disappointed. I wish he'd done better, for the sake of his daughter. However, I can hold these feelings tenderly within the divine light, because it's my reminder to help other people, so I can contribute to a world with fewer parents who are addicts. This is my way of ensuring that Jason's death was not in vain, and of doing right by him.

If I could go back in time and talk to Jason in those last few weeks before he died, I would say something like, "You're going to die and we can't change that, but there's a mysterious interconnectedness to human existence that

I want you to know about. There's going to be a woman named Amy who comes to me a few years from now. She'll share the story of how she had a gun to her own head, and how she chose to live and contribute to the healing of all five of her kids in the process. Even though you're going to choose death, and even though you left while you were in the darkness, it will come back around as light because of what I choose to do with the sadness of losing you . . . because of how I'll choose to transmute the darkness I experienced through that loss. I want you to know, Jason, that I won't just leave it at your death. I'll make something beautiful. I'll plant different seeds."

So you see, even when someone's life is cut short, there is always going to be some part of them that lives in the light. All of us have an eternal essence that continues to live on. Jason's essence lives on in me today through my commitment to transmuting the pain of the choices he made. When I became clear that some part of his eternal essence was living and breathing through me, I realized this wasn't a part of *my* divine light alone; it was also a part of *his*. A sense of awe and wonder washed over me with this realization. Tragedy can give birth to beauty, and the legacy a person was unable to pass on when they were alive can absolutely emerge after their death.

Understanding our experience as humans is a part of our soul evolution. The problems start to occur when we fail to transmute those experiences into light. I could have sat in the pinprick of my perceptions around survivor's guilt, versus the bigger story of what I could commit to in loving memory of my friend. However, I chose my divine story; that is, I chose to move from darkness into light.

Even when the human story and the human experience are riddled with pain and a sense of separation from the divine, our understanding that light is the core of who we are and what we are meant to realize can re-center us in coherence. From this place, we start to see that light is all-encompassing. We also start to see that the divine story is one that persists, in this lifetime and beyond it.

## THE FREQUENCY OF DIVINE LOVE

Not surprisingly, love is at the center of everything I do, and while it's not quite the Is energy, it's very close to it. The way I explain it, one of the highest energies on the planet is divine, unconditional love. In fact, the divine frequency we need on this planet, if it can be summed up in one word, is *love*. We all know this on the deepest levels, but the frequency of love has been distorted by the human story of limitation. Divine love is wildly different and breathtakingly unconditional, because it helps us to see ourselves with both clarity and compassion. The reason this is so important is that we have a tendency to delude ourselves out of knowing the full truth of who we are; we've been taught that the truth hurts, or that it will show us things that make us feel even more shameful and afraid than we already are.

One of the archetypes of unconditional love that we're familiar with is the love of a mother. Of course, there are plenty of mothers who fall short of that paradigm of divine love, but in its highest expression, mother energy is capable of seeing all aspects of a person—their healed and unhealed parts, their light and their shadow—and loving them all the same. (And this motherly paradigm has nothing to do with gender; for example, Oliver was my first experience of that love!)

In the times when I've been able to give myself genuine love—because, after all, it really begins with us—I've felt an overwhelming sense of compassion for myself that has allowed me to understand why I chose pain to begin with. The reason love is so important in achieving coherence is that it helps us feel a sense of deep union with ourselves. In this delicate process of growth, love allows us to greet the stunted parts of ourselves, and to love them back into wholeness.

Coherence is what allows us to recognize that we are a part of the divine, and it is a part of us—and love is the state of being that helps us come into this harmonious unity. That's why I find myself constantly expressing it to every soul I come in contact with.

A man named Brandon came to one of my events and shared that he felt resistant to my effusive expression of love. "I hate it when you tell everyone you love them," he admitted. "How could that possibly be true? You don't even know us!"

He was referring to one of the taglines on my website: "In case no one's told you today, I love you." And I mean it every time!

Brandon went on to say, "*Love* feels like such a sacred word to me, so I don't know how you can use it so lightly."

Brandon was speaking to the fact that we are taught to withhold love from ourselves and others until and unless whomever we're dealing with has proven themselves worthy. Most of us have been taught that love is sacred, but the funny thing is, for some reason the "sacredness" is defined as being a limited resource! It's not a philosophy that makes a whole lot of sense to me. Certainly, not everyone I meet is going to become my partner or best friend, which are relationships defined by co-alignment and shared values—but to me, that absolutely doesn't mean I can't love everyone . . . especially if love is the experience of living in one's light!

Brandon and I went back and forth for a little, so I could clarify what I meant and he could get a chance to share his feelings and ways of defining love. Finally, when I realized that we weren't getting anywhere and that Brandon was adamant about remaining in a state of resistance, I (very lovingly!) said, "I encourage you to hang out for a bit and just feel what it's like to be in a space of love. I'll do my best to embody that frequency of love, so you'll see what I mean. And I look forward to the day you're sharing all that beautiful love inside you in a way that feels safe to you!"

Two days later, at the end of the weekend, Brandon stepped forward because he had something to say. His eyes filled with heartfelt tears, and his voice vibrated with authenticity as he spoke three little words: "I love you." I could feel that he meant it too. He had experienced a healthy, unconditional form of love that asked and expected nothing of him, and it had helped him to see something important: all of his previous perceptions of love had been conditional. He had been taught that love wasn't something you were allowed to give very often, otherwise people would hurt or disrespect you. In the space of two days, he came to see that love was part of his essence—and, honestly, it was everywhere!

And this is what I want you to feel, without a doubt, every moment of your life, dear reader. I want love to be your dominant frequency, so that you always know it's here in abundance. When you really get this, any limiting beliefs about scarcity or "worth" will fly out the window. The darkness will be overcome by light. It is the energy of love that has infused the very writing of this book; my hope is that you're experiencing the frequency of love right now, so that you undoubtedly know and feel it pulsating in your heart, permeating the room you're in.

The amazing thing is, you don't have to understand the first thing about what this love is, or why you're feeling it. The desire to "understand" is just the mind trying to control. The heart knows what coherence is, so it's automatically attuned to the energy of love, even though we might have all kinds of obstacles we place along our own path.

Claudia is a client who found me on the day of her planned suicide attempt. She attended one of my live events. She asked me a question, and I did my best to answer her with my full presence and attention. Little did I know that the few minutes we shared saved her life. She told me this months later, after she experienced a radical shift that she attributed to the love she'd felt from me. She joined my practitioner certification program, and the breakthroughs continued to happen, one after the other. She was in the process of honoring herself and speaking her truth like she'd never done before, which helped remove her from abusive people who didn't allow her to express her beautiful light. What I had reflected to Claudia was simply the truth—that she, and every single one of us, was made in divine perfection.

Even when we're convinced by our human story that we're broken, damaged, and beyond repair, this is never true. I repeat—*never*. No matter how far down the rabbit hole of despair we feel we've fallen, just as Claudia found, we are not the person we've sometimes been taught to believe we are: helpless, small, insignificant . . . and the worst one of all—unworthy of love. These stories block us from the light, but only when we believe them.

Coherence is
what allows us to
recognize that we are
a part of the divine,
and it is a part of us—
and love is the state
of being that helps
us come into this
harmonious unity.

Like I've already said, our culture has a lot of spurious ideas about what love is and isn't. There was a time when I hadn't yet reached the frequency of unconditional love, so I didn't really get it. I thought it meant self-sacrifice and manipulation. I also believed it was only important in intimate relationships. Like Brandon, I thought it was sacred—even though my definition of "sacred" meant it was in short supply and couldn't be given to just anyone. But then, I came into a place where I recognized that we literally come from love. As creations of the divine, we are the embodiment of love. And when we practice being divine love, we experience how wildly freeing and healing it is—without us even having to do or say anything! All we have to do is be, and the ripple effects will be felt, just as Claudia experienced.

That said, divine love can be as ferocious in its expression as it needs to be! Remember, love is not the same as letting someone violate your boundaries. Love isn't even about "feeling better." It's about coming into a state of wholeness wherein you can no longer live in a victim mentality or see yourself as anything other than the brilliant, divine being you are! It's about freeing yourself from any delusions that keep you stuck on autopilot.

A good friend of mine, Kelly, was at my house, sharing about a money block that she'd had for as long as she could remember. It was extremely painful for her, as the block had resulted in the loss of friends, family members, jobs, and even her home. She and I had worked together to address the underlying causes of the block, and I'd sat in countless sessions with her in an attempt to support her healing. Something about the way she was speaking the same words I'd heard before, almost as if she'd memorized a script, made me stop her before she could say anything more.

"Kelly, we've been over this before," I firmly said. "I'm not revisiting this topic. I've helped you plant the seed, water it, and give it sunlight; now, it's your turn to nurture it until it grows. If it grows and where it grows will be on you. I'm done talking about this, because it's not in the highest good."

Kelly wasn't pleased about this. In fact, it brought up all her triggers around feeling abandoned by the people she loved. Certainly, there was a part of me that felt horrible to see my friend suffering, but I also knew the greatest act of love I could offer her in that moment was to empower her—especially because it was clear that she was attempting to give her power away by pretending she was helpless. That's why she was seeking my advice for the umpteenth time. In addition, she didn't really seem to want to do anything to change her situation, as she hadn't listened to any of the advice I'd previously offered. To keep my energy from being drained and to keep her from persisting in the lie that she was powerless, I had to say, "Enough is enough!" I had to set a boundary. I had experienced the same thing with my dad. I needed to get to the point where I was willing to say, "I love you so much that I can't help you."

This is true for all of us. Expressing love is not about expressing codependency or the need for another person's approval. Sometimes, love requires us to do things that might look cruel or hurtful, but none of these are actually done in the frequency of cruelty or the intention to hurt another. Divine love asks that we soulfully do our part while holding others to the highest version of themselves, rather than playing into the not-so-great version, which is eager (consciously or unconsciously) to energetically hijack us and rob us of our own power. As I discussed in Chapter 4, standing in our soul means we choose love over convenience, truth over placating. In other words, we choose the light.

Holding someone else to the fire of love and making them accountable to the highest version of themselves is one of the greatest acts of love we could possibly give another person. Amazingly, Kelly was able to later see this when she realized that what she'd been asking for was the people-pleasing part of me (in other words, an unhealed part of me that was no longer around!) to placate her and come save the day. She'd even gone so far as to burst into tears when I lovingly called her out, because she knew that was one of the triggers my inner people pleaser responded to. "I'm so grateful that you didn't allow me to continue to act out that toxic old pattern of feeling sorry for myself," Kelly said.

When we view ourselves and others through the eyes of love, this helps us and them to step into coherence. The frequency of divine love isn't about "idiot compassion," which is letting someone else walk all over us because we're afraid of conflict. It's about seeing all parts of us and them with the light of clarity. This actually takes us out of pity, people-pleasing, or any of the emotions we tend to confuse for love. Love doesn't shrink or package itself into a more "pleasing" version. It doesn't come out of its high vibration when it shines its light on the wholeness of another being. It is constant and persistent. It is what gently—and sometimes, not so gently!—ushers us into the greatest breakthroughs of our lives.

## Reflection Questions

1. What are the models of love you grew up with? What are some of the things you were taught to believe about love (e.g., it's a "sacred" limited resource, you can only love your close friends and family, etc.)? How have these ideas transformed over time?

2. What does the frequency of divine, unconditional love feel like to you? Don't think about this too hard—rather, step into your heart and let yourself truly connect with it, as it is already a part of who you are. How might this form of love be different from what you were conditioned to believe about love?

3. Think about a time when you were unloving to yourself about something you did. This lack of love might have come through harsh words or self-punishing actions, or something else. Now, through the eyes and frequency of love, offer yourself something different. With the light and clarity of love, what do you now see about your situation that you didn't back then? How do you choose to honor yourself now, despite the choices you made back then?

4. Is there a place in your life where you or someone else could use the "tough" form of unconditional love? Be honest with yourself. Even if you don't necessarily act on giving that form of love (especially if you have an inner,

unhealed people-pleasing part), what would the fire-breathing version of divine love have to say in this situation?

## PEOPLE OF THE LIGHT

Like most people, my human story has caused me to occasionally get stuck in thoughts like "I hurt that person," or "That person hurt me." However, in a state of coherence, I quickly move into the bigger picture, which helps me to transform these mistakes into wisdom. These days, my capacity to be in coherence is so strong that I can genuinely offer love to people who have done the most heinous things. This doesn't bypass accountability; rather, love is what helps us to be accountable to ourselves and others. Love is one of the most powerful forces in the universe because it sheds light on anything we call "evil." Evil is simply that which has forgotten it is light.

I'll often get questions of a metaphysical nature from students and clients, especially when it comes to the nature of evil and darkness. They wonder, "If the divine is all about goodness and light, why is there so much evil and darkness in the world?"

Of course, this is a question that spiritual teachers across time and space have dealt with. The way I explain it is, if we look at darkness and fear, we can do so on both a micro and a macro level. On a micro level, we can take the example of someone who abuses others. Such a person holds a lot of darkness, and the only way they can maintain their energy or sense of power is by victimizing others. Their concept of power is inherently limited; they can't see that source energy is infinite and available to all of us, because they view power from a base material level, as a resource that is in short supply. In a strange way, their victim is the source of light from which they derive a sense of power. The ability to change this toxic dynamic lies in the abuser's victim, who can put an end to the cycle of darkness because, ironically, they are the one who holds the true power.

On a macro level, all of us recognize the darkness that lives in our world, which exists in the form of war, poverty, sex trafficking, terrorism, and so many horrendous acts that remove us from the light. However, this darkness has no genuine, self-contained power. It's just that the darkness has learned how to hijack the light and feed off of it. However, if those of us who are committed to living in the light can remain in our light, against the odds, the darkness cannot overpower us.

Let me explain how this might work. Let's say someone who is committed to living in the light watches the news and feels debilitated by the images and stories that flash before their eyes. They're overwhelmed by what they see, which doesn't feel like it's in resonance with who they are on the most fundamental levels. They are overwhelmed, sad, and afraid for their family and humanity in general. In such a situation, the darkness (the presence of evil in the world) is sucking energy out of the light once again. This is why we must be absolutely committed to raising our vibration whenever we encounter darkness.

I've had people say to me, "Well, Mandy, that's easy for you to say, because you already live a great life!" And while that's true—hello! Have you heard me talk about my past? Despite all I've been through, at some point I made the conscious decision to transmute my feelings of sadness, powerlessness, and fear, because I came to understand that I was just feeding the darkness.

As always, the power is within us because that's where the light ultimately lives. We are all fractals of divine consciousness, and wherever we direct our human consciousness collectively determines the next move we end up making on the chessboard of human existence. This is why it's absolutely imperative that we focus on the good, the positive, the divine. Because we are co-creative beings, we have the ability to manipulate matter and existence itself. It's only when we accidentally give our power away, cause a divide, and separate from the divine that we focus on what we do *not* want in our world—on that which makes us feel sad, scared, and powerless. This is why we must be extremely conscious of where and how we direct our energy. We must not give in to fear (or the 24/7 news cycle, for that matter!) or mindless consumption. Directing our consciousness toward what we want (e.g., love, peace, harmony, more connection, and dialogue across our differences) helps us to better hone our intentions— and that which we do not want simply ceases to exist. This is how we can come to heal the human story of separation and fully unite with the divine.

If darkness were all there was (which is what a lot of people on the planet mistakenly believe), it would not be able to exist. Without morality, values, and the desire to make the world a better place, darkness would eventually consume and destroy itself.

And what if the world were filled with predominantly light? Well then, the world would flourish! People of the light, who know they are here to do good and to spread the energy of love and harmony, would enable the world to discover and live up to its true potential. To fill the world with light, however, we must be aware of the ways we can start to do this in micro (in our daily personal lives) and macro (in our way of relating to humanity and the planet as a whole) ways. When we truly attend to the little and big pictures, we recognize that empowering ourselves to know, live inside, and source from the light rather than lending it to darkness can help us to eradicate the darkness altogether! And we don't even have to "fight" that darkness! The energy of fighting—at least, when it isn't a pure, neutral energy that comes from a space of love and true empowerment—actually lends itself to depletion by the force of darkness. This is why wars (whether they're between nations, family members, or even different parts of the self), though they may seem to be justifiable through our human lens, only lead to the proliferation of darkness.

I've come up close and personal with many different manifestations of darkness, as I've had my fair share of working with survivors of extremely traumatic experiences. I specifically recall a time when sex trafficking was finally becoming a more mainstream topic, and there was a great deal of global discussion about it (which, let's be real, needed to happen). But when the topic was being spotlighted, I went through a two-week period of barely being able to function. I was totally debilitated and drained. I've felt such a deep connection to global consciousness ever since I was a little girl, and given the work I do in the world, I could feel the darkness of the collective experience settling around me, even if I wasn't reading or watching the news. I've worked closely with victims of trafficking with great success, but there was something about this period of time that caused me to emulate the feelings a lot of people go through when they're exposed to the brutal realities of such a crime. I'd also started to work with a direct-intervention organization focused on trafficking that does amazing work in bringing freedom and healing to victims of human trafficking and sexual exploitation. As I sat with the extent of the suffering that human trafficking had created on this planet, I was *pissed*. There was a part of me that wanted to fight to aggressively protect all the children who had been harmed. However, there was nothing empowering about my experience. I became paralyzed by my anger and frustration, to the extent that I felt incapacitated. I couldn't help but feel like I was staring into the jaws of darkness, and there was no way out. I didn't know how to confront a problem that was this big.

One day, as I was talking to my friend Grace, I confided in her and said, "For the first time in a long time, I just don't know what I'm supposed to do. It's obviously getting my attention for a reason, and I feel like I need to go out and fight this. But I'm not sure how I'm being called into action, because I'm so unclear and foggy about all of it."

Grace looked me straight in the eye and said, "You know, Mandy, this probably isn't what you want to hear, but I'll say it, anyway. Know your place."

"Excuse me?" I didn't know what she was getting at.

"You help people get out of those dark tunnels. *That's* your place. And not only that, but the majority of your work and purpose in the world is to bring in so much light that the darkness doesn't even exist. There are people out there whose job it is to fight, to go into the tunnels to save the children. But that's not your place, so that's why it feels so heavy. So, I'm saying to know your place, so that you can shine your light to the greatest capacity and help the greatest number of people."

I was deeply humbled and grateful for Grace's words. I knew then and there from the release I felt in my heart that she was right. The darkness had debilitated me to the point where I couldn't shine my light. So, of course, it had done exactly what it had always wanted; it had shut down the light. I realized I couldn't fight that energy with anger, which was weakening me rather than strengthening my resolve to do something. What I had to do was lean further into the light and keep shining as brightly as I could, so I could then help others to do the same. My mission and purpose is the healing of the planet at a root level, and I have always done this by living inside the frequency of love, so that the type of darkness that is tied to brutal realities like human trafficking simply can't exist.

All of us hold both the light and the darkness within ourselves, but coherence asks not that we fight with and subdue the darkness; it asks that we transmute the darkness so that we can bring it back to divine light. Darkness is ultimately neither good nor bad in the larger scope of things; it's what we do with the darkness, the heaviness, the evil, that determines our personal and collective outcomes.

### Reflection Questions

1. Have there been times in your life when you encountered what some might call the energy of "evil"? In thinking about these situations now, can you recognize or entertain the idea that evil is just light that has forgotten itself? Be honest with yourself here, and compassionately sit with any triggers or strong feelings that might be coming up. (If the feelings are strong, this might be a good place to practice the pattern interrupt process you learned at the end of Chapter 6.)

2. Have you ever felt confused, scared of, or angry
   with the darkness in the world at large, or in
   your own personal encounters? How did you
   move through those feelings?

3. How strong is your own commitment to
   living in the light? How can you hold the
   bigger picture of darkness and light, without
   succumbing to darkness?

## NO . . . NOT EVERYTHING IS "PERFECT"

One erroneous idea I'm always quick to correct is the
idea that understanding coherence is equivalent to saying,
"If coherence is about all that is, maybe the big picture is
more complex than we give it credit for. And maybe on
some divine level, everything is actually perfect, even the
stuff that's difficult."

This is a common misconception, and here's why. The
tendency to equate coherence with unconditional acceptance of everything that's happening can sometimes be
distorted into a moral relativism that suggests everything
is "shades of gray" that are part of the bigger picture—that
all of it has a place. On a certain level, this is true in that
everything we encounter is an opportunity to move back
into alignment with the divine. However, we have to be
very careful about where our perception is coming from: Is
it from a desire to realign with the highest vibration, or to
justify and romanticize terrible decisions and situations,
and remain stuck within them?

Remember, it all comes down to free will. If someone
chooses to jump out the window of a multistory building
and breaks their back, that came from a human choice,

not a divine one. And if someone decides to stay in a toxic relationship with an abusive partner because they insist that person is their twin flame and heartache is part of the lesson they're integrating, that wasn't God's will—it was the will of the person who made that choice, perhaps out of a mistaken belief that the amplitude of love they feel is equal to the amplitude of suffering the relationship entails.

Our experiences are meant to teach us valuable lessons about ourselves, and the nature of reality. However, we sometimes fail to learn those lessons and to transmute the darkness into the light (as I was able to transmute my story of survivor's guilt about Jason into one that helped me recognize my own capacity to help others in the way I hadn't been able to help him). This is how we get stuck in situations that are neither wise nor sustainable. Sometimes— because this is a freewill universe—we choose pain and it has a valuable lesson to teach us. But at what point will we learn the lesson so that we can expand our consciousness and move into new, high-vibrational experiences that help us to embrace our divine light? Just as it's our choice to get stuck in a loop of the same emotional state, it's also our choice whether or not we continue to attract the same traumatic experiences rather than allow them to return us to wholeness.

It's true that nonjudgmental acceptance of a situation can connect us to our divine light in a powerful way; however, this is not the same as saying, "I'm okay with staying in this situation forever." When we're in the flow of the universe, even in our moments of loss and pain, we can see the possibility of a more complete way of being in the world. We can say, "This is the painful thing I'm going through right now, but I know there's more than this, and

I'm allowing myself to surrender to divine flow to take me to where I need to be." The light actually expands our menu of options.

Some of the choices we make, even if they're a part of our larger story, didn't happen because it was all in divine order. The soulful journey includes wrong turns and unnecessary pain, and we can see this with respect to the larger human story that is unfolding, which is rife with darkness—not because the divine willed it, but because our limited understanding of reality brought it into being. I'm not saying this to give you another excuse to beat yourself up over what went wrong. Remember, the divine is not a punishing judge standing over you and delivering black-and-white verdicts. It is an energy of light, love, and acceptance that stewards us into higher levels of consciousness when we surrender to it.

Ultimately, it is what we do with the lessons that emerged from all the wrong turns that determines whether we step into our divine light, or whether we get caught in a dark web of our human choices.

## Reflection Questions

1. Have you ever attributed the pain and suffering in your life to divine will rather than human will? How has this perception served or hindered you?

2. Have you ever used "It's complicated," or "Everything's perfect, if you look at the bigger picture," as an excuse to stay stuck in less-than-favorable situations, or to justify ill treatment?

3. Can you identify any lessons in your life that you may be resistant to fully integrating so that you can move into a higher vibration?

## THE RAINBOW OF YOU

Coherence brings us into a radical acceptance of the self, which includes all of our facets, whether we perceive them as "good" or "bad." As Oliver likes to say to me, "I love the rainbow of you, Mandy." It's such a beautiful sentiment, especially when we learn to apply it to ourselves—because, as we come into greater coherence with who we are, we bring more of our light into the world, and we also learn to remain in our light so that we cannot be knocked off our stable base.

This requires looking at all parts of who we are (and that includes all our perceived poor decisions and mistakes) with divine clarity and saying, "I understand you. I hear you. And I love you," not, "You aren't what I need you to be, so you have to change," which is all too often the message we absorb from the external world. The thing is, the external world only reflects our fragmented state of being. Most of us are walking around with this idea that we can only embrace the shiniest, prettiest, smartest, and best parts of who we are, and we need to push everything else down. But when we do that, we miss the opportunity to lovingly bring all parts of ourselves into coherence so that we're standing fully in the light. Because so many of our parts are shrouded in darkness and shame, we can't help but vibrate this frequency in the world, which impacts the collective experience of light.

When people get confused about this, I say, "Think about the way you'd talk to a child. Would you tell them they're bad or stupid, and they need to change in order to be loved?" Most people are shocked by the mere idea (although, sadly, this is what many of us also grow up with). "Okay," I continue, "but can you see that you're doing this to yourself! You're telling these parts of you that are looking for your approval, just like a child might, that they need to change in order to be loved. If you really think about it, that's just another form of abuse."

When we begin to understand and put our entire lives into a greater context, we can offer ourselves the salve of our own love. We start to see that things we did or said that we might never do or say today, or the personality quirks that embarrass us or make us feel "less than," are aspects of the self that need our tenderness, not our judgment. Sometimes, we discover that the parts we dislike are actually unrecognized strengths; other times, as we hold them up to the light, we see they were just coping mechanisms meant to help us get through the day. If we can eliminate self-judgment and be courageous enough to consider that just maybe we misunderstood ourselves, divine love cannot help but rush in, because it has always been there—it's just that we built a strong dam that kept its cleansing waters from breaking through.

Coherence and wholeness can sometimes come to us from the people we love. When I met Oliver, I realized that for the first time in my life, I could just be Mandy—the goofy, wild, funny, soulful, heartfelt, complex version of me that I couldn't seem to be with most people. This sense of absolute familiarity was a godsend, because it helped me to come home inside my own heart, which enabled me to radiate my authenticity even more brightly.

Embracing the full rainbow of who we are also emerges when we're attuned to all aspects of our personal gifts in such a way that there's nothing that can get between us and the divine. We're living and breathing light. As I've mentioned, our own misconceptions can get in the way of that clear channel. For example, at a young age, I would see and hear "energies" that nobody else seemed to notice. This frightened me, which caused me to shut off my special gift. But years later, I began to build my programs by sitting quietly and asking what the world needed. In this way, I started to channel information that came from my connection to the divine realm of spirit. In truth, I am a walking channel most of the time, and I don't recall half the things I say when I'm in deep service. Today, I'm willing to walk the world in this pure, immediate state—even though I had no context for it when I was a kid, and no way to really hone and direct that talent. Channeling continued to show up throughout my life, and I continued to push it down.

Things shifted enormously when I met Oliver, who is known as the Spiritual Activator (I kid you not—people's gifts literally activate when they're in his presence!). We were driving together one night, and when I looked at the stars, something magical happened. I began to talk about love in a voice that wasn't even mine, and to share a beautiful, expansive perspective about humanity and where we were headed. This was not Mandy in her human story—it was me connecting to something incredibly mystical and divine. Oliver comes from a long lineage of healers in the Philippines, so nothing that was happening felt surprising or out of the ordinary to him. For the first time, as I basked in Oliver's loving attention and approval, I recognized that what I had was a gift rather than a curse. Love was lubricating all the light that was pouring through me. I knew that it was pure, safe, and sacred, so I began using that gift to spread a message of wholeness and healing. Not to mention, the mere act of taking the gift I'd been given at an early age and honoring it actually changed the frequency of my past. Because we experience coherence in the present, divine time-bending happens in spades—we start to see the past and future through an awareness that helps us to realize none of it is a mistake in the eyes of divine love. It's all just there to be offered to the light. We start to grab hold of the cosmic download in ways that make us more capable of matching our world with the frequency of the divine.

Trust me, that kind of cosmic download is much easier and smoother when we stop running away from ourselves. At a certain point, I realized I could no longer do this, because if I continued to, it would kill me. I'd just keep fragmenting until there was nothing authentic left. At a certain point, I sat in deep silence and inwardly said to myself, "All the things I've experienced and all the poor decisions I've made, I fully surrender to the divine. I fully love and accept all these parts of my human story." Of course, Oliver had granted me the experience of what self-love could look like, simply through the vibration of his own unconditional acceptance of me. His love helped me realize something: if another person could recognize my divine perfection even in my ugliest moments, I had no right to continue to mistreat myself. I had to step up and embody that same divine love.

I can still recall what happened next. I sat in my meditation room and called forth the infinite versions of me—from this life, as well as all other dimensions and realities. Each version of Mandy was a little different from the next one. Some of the versions were bright and spectacular, and others were more closed-off. I felt enormous love for every single one, and I had the sense that it was my responsibility to bring them all together. I wanted more than anything else to love them all, even the versions that seemed stunted. I said to this colorful array of Mandys, "We're moving forward! Everyone who wants to come along on this incredible journey, let's do this!"

In my mind's eye, they started blending into one cohesive version of Mandy. I could feel the healed and unhealed parts of me coming together into a rapturous and contained whole. It was one of the most beautiful experiences of my life. But suddenly, the view changed and I found myself in a dark dungeon. There, I saw a Mandy who had been hidden away for God knows how long. In fact, this Mandy didn't even look like me—if I had to compare her to anyone, it would be Gollum from the *Lord of the Rings* movies. She was decrepit, with dull, gray skin, and she sat crouched in a corner, malnourished and frightened. I gently asked her, "Are you going to come?" She told me that she couldn't—at least, not in this current version of who she was. I sat with her, with the utmost patience and love, not attempting to change a thing. Finally, she dissipated and turned into golden dust. I realized this was her way of transmuting so that she could actually become a part of the experience. It seemed like the death of that old decrepit Mandy was required so the beautiful light that lived deep inside her could come along and be part of the experience of this grand adventure called life—so she could resurrect as the most authentic and coherent Mandy there could be.

## PRACTICE: THE RAINBOW OF YOU

1. Find a quiet, comfortable spot where you can sit or lie down for at least 30 minutes, without interruptions. Feel free to light candles or incense, and call in the divine light or any other support you need.

2. When you're ready, head over to discoverthepromise.com/meditation where you can download a special meditation I created just for you. Take a few deep, grounding breaths before you hit "play." Set an intention to come into coherence by embracing the rainbow of you and gathering together all the beautiful versions of yourself: past, present, and future.

3. Welcome whatever comes up during the meditation. Take time to journal about your experience afterward, and be oh, so gentle with yourself. Drink lots of water and treat yourself with extra TLC. If you find that you have to come back to the meditation more than once, that's okay. Just continue to set the intention that you are choosing coherence and light.

## YOUR DIVINE LIGHT PRACTICE

Work with *the Rainbow of You* practice as many times as you wish. It's a beautiful ritual that will help you to bring all your beautiful parts into coherence, and to recognize that you are inherently lovable and inherently whole.

As always, take time to revisit the reflection questions at the end of each section in this chapter, and to journal on them.

## Takeaways

1. The final pathway of light, **coherence**, is the supreme frequency of all that is. Coherence allows us to integrate all the different elements of our lives—including our human and divine stories. It endows us with a sense of awe and wonder as we reconnect with the bigger picture and the mystery of existence.

2. One of the highest energies on the planet is divine, unconditional love. Unfortunately, the frequency of love has been distorted and seen through the fogged-up lens of the human story of limitation and scarcity. Divine love is wildly different and breathtakingly unconditional, in that it helps us to see ourselves with both clarity and compassion.

3. Evil is just light that has forgotten itself. While darkness and evil are realities on this planet, they are not more powerful than the light, which has the ability to transmute darkness. On both the micro and macro levels, those of us who have made a commitment to live in the light can conquer the darkness—by recognizing when we've stepped into the frequency of fear and deciding that we're going to operate within the frequency of love instead.

4.  Seeing the vast scope of divine light and everything it is capable of holding should never be used as an excuse for harmful choices and behaviors. In other words, rather than being part of the "perfection" of divine light, many painful experiences are unnecessary wrong turns we took due to our limited human perception and miscalculated choices.

5.  Coherence brings us into a radical acceptance of the self, which includes every last part of who we are. When we learn to embrace the beautiful rainbow of our complex being, we come into greater coherence and become more capable of radiating light into our neglected parts and into the world.

# conclusion

Dear beautiful soul,

Congratulations! You've been on a beautiful journey through the seven pathways that will help you to access all the Promise has to offer you. Although the principles may seem separate from one another at first glance, they are part of a single unified truth. They're part of a promise woven into the very fabric of life that you are so intimately connected to as an infinite, divine being having a finite, human experience.

Even in the times you may have felt alone and lost in the deepest and darkest caverns of your most painful human experiences, you really weren't. This is the heart-felt promise that the divine light makes to us every single day of our lives. Inevitably, some moments may feel easier to remember and call forth the frequency of the Promise, but the more you come back to this book and let the energy soak into you, the faster and easier it will be to embrace. I know it will become your new normal if you continue to explore the Promise with an open mind and heart. Remember, though, we were also gifted with free will, so we must be the ones who take the first step toward the light. My hope is that this book has put some wind in your sails and given you the courage that is necessary to continue the voyage. I pray the energy of the words that I have been a vessel for touches your soul and brings you back to truth. May the Promise feel familiar in your divine soul, yet new in your human perspective. And if you ever feel yourself lost in the maze of your human story, you can always come back to these pages; you can choose to read from the very beginning, select a chapter that calls to you, or even open the book at random to synchronistically find the sentence or paragraph that wants to bring you home to your true essence. As I wrote these words, I prayed the energy of these concepts will touch you so deeply, that you will be forever changed, even if you can not consciously understand why things are beginning to feel . . . "different."

You can also come back to the reflection questions and exercises whenever you need to be reminded of what you already know, deep down. Taking those precious moments to check in with yourself are immeasurably impactful. But just know that there's no specific formula for stepping into the light within. I didn't write this book as a series of linear steps to get "there." That doesn't reflect life, and unless you're baking a cake, too specific of steps tend to slow us down in this journey. Let your life be a constant expansion in all directions, never ending, just like the universe. In fact, there's no final destination, since the light is always here with you—and finding it can take an instant or a lifetime. It's up to you.

Every single pathway in this book contains the rest, just like every human experience exists within the divine experience. So, even if you choose to linger on just one pathway, you will ultimately find yourself visiting the others. And as you integrate the tools and prompts into your life, you'll find yourself weaving your own uniquely gorgeous approach to embracing the light—with all the heart and grace that are yours to wield. You won't ever feel that you need to lean back on an intellectual construct or template for accessing the light, because you'll naturally develop the confidence and competence to catalyze the gifts that are part of your true nature. Best of all, you'll get to experience the juiciness and richness of this incredible, infinitely creative human realm without any old, disempowering beliefs to hinder your progress. I want to see you shining brightly, and I know it's within your capacity to do so!

Of course, the path of finding the light isn't a one-and-done deal. It's something we access through every choice we make, every action we take, every word we speak, every thought we think. The ancient sage Lao Tzu is credited with saying: "Watch your thoughts, they become your words. Watch your words, they become your actions. Watch your actions, they become your habits. Watch your habits, they become your character. Watch your character, it becomes your destiny."

When we step into our divine light, we access the evolutionary aspects of our human destiny. We weren't meant to suffer on this planet—to be stuck in patterns of lack, greed, and disconnection that keep us from knowing and realizing our potential. I know this can feel really hard to accept, especially because it seems like suffering is all around us and has been the norm since time immemorial. However, sages like Lao Tzu, as well as people from all walks of life, have tapped into the truth: we have the power to transmute all suffering and to welcome the light of the divine to shine on every seemingly insurmountable obstacle that stands in our way.

Again, this isn't about overhauling your humanness and pretending life is without issues. The light has so much room and infinite patience for our messiness—in fact, it welcomes it! And when we start looking at our human story from a divine perspective, everything changes. (And I offer myself up as Exhibit A!)

I encourage you to try any of the tools in this book for the next 30 days, which you might want to stretch into a few months (especially if you're having fun, which is also the divine's intention!). If you've been struggling with feelings of not-enoughness, despair, powerlessness, or simply a case of the blahs that make it really hard to love your life and step into your purpose, I encourage you to turn the principles in this book into daily habits that inform your destiny! I've seen it enough times to know that you could be living a completely different story—one that lets you be calm, poised, and empowered, so that you radiate unconditional love. Seriously, even if you move 1 percent in the direction of the light, as we explored in Chapter 6, you'll experience major transformations—in the form of both tiny metaphorical earthquakes and huge volcanic eruptions that create new, lush landmasses in your life!

Often, those major shifts are less about the "externals" in your life—the people, places, objects, and situations that your light will certainly magnetize and manifest— but rather, an internal sense of peace and connection to your higher self.

I remember sitting in my house in Laguna Beach, asking Oliver the following question: "If you were at the end of the road, how would you know for certain that you'd lived a happy and abundant life?" We both refer to this phase as "getting to the rocking chair," and it's something we often talk about—not in a morbid way, but in one that helps us to never take our decisions for granted or lose sight of the big picture.

As he shared his life intentions, he then asked me the same.

I closed my eyes and felt the warmth of divine light surrounding my heart. I smiled as I said, with the utmost certainty, "I would know I'd lived the best life possible if I felt God's presence in everything I did."

If you'd asked me that same question years ago, before my knees-to-the-earth, dark-night-of-the-soul breakthrough, I would probably have given you a very different answer—most likely, one that was focused on specific measurements, such as how many people I had helped, how many resources I'd left my children, and how much recognition I received from the world at large. But in my own sacred walk toward the light, I can now see that what I do or don't do is totally beside the point. I could be riding a bike, baking bread, creating a business, or teaching people to heal their trauma—the bottom line is, when we feel and sense the divinity in everything in and around us, we have already unlocked the light that makes life worth living.

You don't need to check all the boxes or fulfill a narrow perception of what happiness looks like. In fact, those perceptions may change altogether once you tap into the treasures that await you inside the divine light. The only goal from that vantage point is to connect with the divine within everything as often as you possibly can. Everything else will take care of itself.

I do my best to live in the light and embrace what the Promise has shown me—which helps us all to navigate the complexity of life with a pure heart that is willing to surrender its protective armor in order to touch the awe-inspiring, wonder-filled mystery that infuses absolutely everything. Because when you take a single step toward the divine, it comes rushing back at you with unabated, unconditional love. And that's where the magic begins.

May your life be filled with the kind of magic that far surpasses any fairy-tale ending you could imagine. And let me let you in on a little secret. This Promise I have shared with you? It has never left you. It is there in your darkest moments, it's there when you look in the mirror, it has been with you since the day you were born. Not because it sat beside you, but because it lives within you.

And in case no one has told you today—

I love you,

**Mandy**

# a prayer

I hope this prayer will help you to remember the principles inside *The Promise*, as you honor your own promise to yourself to living in the divine light from this day forward.

I choose to *expand* into the Promise, and embrace my divine light.

*Self-knowledge* frees me from false ideas of who I am and I am made whole again.

I discover *empathy* for myself and others, for all the ways we have limited our full expression as beings of divinity.

I exercise *clarity* as I behold the bigger picture and the awe-inspiring perfection of the universe.

I *transmute* my wounds into my greatest gifts and claim my full value. In doing so, I serve others too.

I follow the path to joy and purpose as I accept my ability to *co-create* with the divine.

I integrate the diverse elements of life into *coherence*, which lets me become a beacon of light for myself and others.

I am light. I am love. I am free.

# acknowledgments

I'd like to thank everyone who contributed to this book, as well as God for filling me up that night on my knees so I could be the vessel of this important understanding of existence.

To Oliver, you have been the most supportive partner in life. Even in my dreams, in every reality, I search for you.

To Braydon, Zion, Malakai, and the children I have lost—you give me deep purpose and proved to me that I do love all of the world as I love each of you.

To Anthony William, for being like a big brother in this walk of service with your guidance and belief in me.

To Mom, for growing with me and telling me I can be anything. I learn about myself through watching you.

To Daddy, your intricacies helped me love my intricacies.

To Billie, for your loving protective sisterhood.

To Chris, for your own service to the world and your Godliness.

To Oliver's family: Claudine, Elaine, Liezl, Pia, and Mary-anne—your embodiment of love makes me so grateful to have you as family.

To Mamas Monica, for teaching me when I was 15 that whenever you are in a position to help someone, you do.

To Melody, Patty, Lindsay, Lizzi, Reid, and all the Hay House family, thank you for your warmth and support in spreading this work I am blessed to do.

To Nirmala Nataraj, your professionalism and ease were a blessing. So grateful for you.

To Dennis, my manager at the scrapyard, for telling me you'd fire me if I didn't reach for more in life on my own.

To Laura Nolan, thank you for taking care of "the details" and championing me through my every endeavor.

To Nikki, Melissa, Jess, Kathy, Jen, Rachelle, Fatou, Wendy, Nicole, Yvonne, Elle, Dianne, Niki, Mike, Sonia, Emily, Stephanie, and all of the Authentic Living Team, Authentic Living Foundation volunteers, and Authentic Living Heartland staff for supporting the work we do and believing so deeply in our mission.

To people in my past and earlier versions of me—thank you for your difficult, painful, and beautiful lessons.

To all the therapists, counselors, and coaches I have certified over the years through the EME Integration Practice, thank you for being a part of the ripple effect.

To the incredible souls I get to call friends—thank you for empowering me, celebrating me, and seeing me.

To all of humanity, it is an honor to serve you in the highest good of all.

# about the author

**Mandy Morris** is the founder of Authentic Living, an educational organization that has more than 4 million students in over 60 countries, with both online and in-person courses designed to help individuals rewire their mind, heart, and energy for total abundance in all aspects of life.

Mandy's science- and love-based methods for creating instant and lasting change have been studied, taught, and used all over the world by therapists and coaches. Her certified coaches practice globally. Mandy worked in Scandinavia and the U.S. to study how an individual's brain patterns changed through her communicative therapy methodology. Mandy works with childhood trauma, sabotaging beliefs, trigger management, abusive relationships, adult trauma, the science of manifesting, and the law of attraction. With her husband, Oliver Niño, she co-founded Hustle & Heart, a philanthropic initiative aimed at providing education, alleviating hunger, stopping childhood trafficking, and providing necessary resources and disaster support throughout the Philippines, U.S., and Africa.

To learn more about Mandy and her work, visit **mandymorris.love** and **@manifestwithmandy** on Instagram.

We hope you enjoyed this Hay House book. If you'd like to receive our online catalog featuring additional information on Hay House books and products, or if you'd like to find out more about the Hay Foundation, please contact:

Hay House, Inc., P.O. Box 5100, Carlsbad, CA 92018-5100
(760) 431-7695 or (800) 654-5126
(760) 431-6948 (fax) or (800) 650-5115 (fax)
www.hayhouse.com® • www.hayfoundation.org

———

*Published in Australia by:* Hay House Australia Pty. Ltd.,
18/36 Ralph St., Alexandria NSW 2015
*Phone:* 612-9669-4299 • *Fax:* 612-9669-4144
www.hayhouse.com.au

*Published in the United Kingdom by:* Hay House UK, Ltd.,
The Sixth Floor, Watson House, 54 Baker Street, London W1U 7BU
*Phone:* +44 (0)20 3927 7290 • *Fax:* +44 (0)20 3927 7291
www.hayhouse.co.uk

*Published in India by:* Hay House Publishers India,
Muskaan Complex, Plot No. 3, B-2, Vasant Kunj, New Delhi 110 070
*Phone:* 91-11-4176-1620 • *Fax:* 91-11-4176-1630
www.hayhouse.co.in

———

Access New Knowledge.
Anytime. Anywhere.

Learn and evolve at your own pace
with the world's leading experts.

www.hayhouseU.com

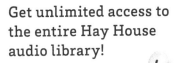